FELICIA
CARTRIGHT
AND THE
KNOTTED WIRE

Felicia   Joan

FELICIA CARTRIGHT

AND THE
KNOTTED WIRE

BERNARD PALMER

ANEKO
PRESS

Cover Artwork: Adobe Firefly, Ideogram
Editor: Charlene Miskimen

Aneko Press Youth

www.anekopress.com

Aneko Press, Life Sentence Publishing, and our logos are trademarks of
Life Sentence Publishing, Inc.
203 E. Birch Street
P.O. Box 652
Abbotsford, WI 54405

JUVENILE FICTION / Religious / Christian / Action & Adventure

Paperback ISBN: 979-8-88936-308-8

eBook ISBN: 979-8-88936-309-5

10 9 8 7 6 5 4 3 2 1

Available where books are sold

CONTENTS

FOREWORD

The events of this story did not really happen, but the book was inspired by the Bible Club Boat on the Centrum Canal in downtown Amsterdam. For a number of years, Anne Punt and Annie Verboom, missionaries under the Bible Club Movement, now known as BCM International, labored there, reaching the children of indifferent parents for Christ.

The Author

CHAPTER 1

THE BIBLE BOAT

Amelia Duncan, the crisp, proper dean of Boston's Wellington School for Girls, sat up as the plane from Geneva nosed through the overcast toward Holland's Schipolt Airport. It was a gray, dreary afternoon. Rain flecked the plane's windows and made the fields below quite soggy. It would probably be cold when they deplaned. But, then, it had been cold every time she had been in Amsterdam. Idly, she wondered if Mabel Cruse and Joka Vanderende would be at the airport to meet them.

"Fasten seat belts," the sign ordered.

Instantly, Miss Duncan became dean again. "Felicia," she said.

The slight, attractive blond girl to her right stirred sleepily.

"Felicia, we're almost in Amsterdam."

"Oh." She squirmed upright in her seat. "So soon?"

Miss Duncan consulted her watch. "No, it is not 'so soon,' as you say. We are exactly on schedule, which means we are neither early nor late."

"Yes, Miss Duncan," Felicia replied dutifully.

"The pilot is asking us to secure our seat belts for the descent."

"Oh," Felicia murmured, still half asleep. "Oh, I see." She fumbled with the stainless steel fastener.

"Now, would you please waken Joan?"

Joan Bailey was sprawling in her seat and resting her dark head against the window, sound asleep. Her seat belt had not been fastened.

"Joan." Felicia touched her friend on the shoulder. "Joan."

No answer.

"Joan!"

Miss Duncan wrinkled her nose distastefully as Felicia's voice rose.

"Miss Cartright, please remember your manners."

Felicia glanced imploringly at their instructor and chaperone. "I'm sorry, Miss Duncan," she said, "but you know how hard it is to get Joan awake."

"Indeed, I do." Her eyes glinted fire. "Miss Bailey!"

Her voice was not loud, but it carried a tone of authority. Joan sat bolt upright.

"I'm sorry, Miss Duncan," she blurted. "I didn't hear the question."

Felicia laughed. "The question is, are you going

to fasten your seat belt, or do you want to bounce on your nose when we land?"

"Oh," Joan blushed as she hurried to secure the belt. "Oh. I was dreaming I was back in Wellington in one of Miss Duncan's classes and–" Her voice trailed away.

"And you were sleeping, as usual," the dean of women added dryly.

Both girls looked quickly at her. Since they had left the States with her early in June, nearly a month and a half before, they hadn't been able to tell when she was serious and when she was teasing them.

Only after both girls had fastened their seat belts did Miss Duncan fasten hers.

In a couple of minutes, they were on the ground, taxiing up to the beautiful big terminal building.

"I certainly hope your friends are here to meet us," Felicia said uneasily.

"You needn't concern yourself about that," Miss Duncan countered. "Mabel is a Wellington girl herself. She knows the importance of being prompt." Her expression softened slightly. "And besides, she was my roommate and very best friend for three entire years at Wellington. She messaged me in Switzerland that she would be here to meet us. I know she will be."

Joan leaned forward to squint out the window.

"The only person I can see out there who fits your description of Miss Cruse has got a little boy by the hand."

"That wouldn't be Mabel!" Miss Duncan retorted primly.

It was only a minute or so until the plane door was opened and the passengers began to file down the ramp into the customs section of the terminal. On the top step of the ramp, Miss Duncan stopped abruptly, her eyes widening.

"It is Mabel!" she exclaimed aloud.

At that instant, the attractive, red-haired woman dropped the hand of the boy by her side and waved excitedly. Miss Duncan waved in return.

In most of the European countries where they had stopped, the customs officials had done little more than ask them a few questions and open a bag or two. Here, however, it was different. The officers were courteous. But the line moved slowly because each bag was being opened and inspected carefully.

Joan poked Felicia in the back.

"What do you suppose this is all about?" she whispered.

Before Felicia could answer, the smiling young customs official was standing before her.

"I am so sorry," he said in broken English, "but I am going to have to ask you to open your bags."

Felicia did as she was told. The official didn't remove her belongings from the suitcase, but he might just as well have. He inspected each piece, taking care not to wrinkle them more than was absolutely necessary. He ran his hand expertly along the lining for telltale lumps that would indicate hidden parcels. Then he asked her to empty her purse so he could give it the same minute examination. Only when he had satisfied himself that she had nothing illicit in her possession did he allow her to close her bags. Then he directed his attention to the suitcases Joan and Miss Duncan set on the counter before him. He went through them with the same thoroughness.

"Thank you very much," he said at last, returning their bags to them. "I am sorry we have to subject you to such inconvenience."

"That's quite all right, young man," Miss Duncan said crisply and without anger. "I know you were doing your duty just now. I have no quarrel with that."

"Thank you. Some travelers are very irritated."

"I can understand that too. As you have seen for yourself, we had nothing to hide. But your actions have made me a bit curious." She lowered her voice. "Tell me, did you really suspect that we had brought goods into your country without declaring it?"

Apologetically, he smiled at her.

"No," he said. "As a matter of fact, I was sure before I even asked you to open your bags that I would find nothing. In this department, we soon learn to judge the people we are examining."

"Then," she continued, "if you don't mind telling me, why was it done?"

His smile broadened.

"You'll have to ask that question of someone in

a higher place of authority than I am. Two weeks ago, we were given orders to search every bag that goes through as thoroughly as though we suspect the owner of smuggling."

Interest glittered in Felicia's blue eyes.

"Are they looking for something special?" she asked.

The official stiffened perceptibly, and in a twinkling, his friendliness was gone.

"That," he retorted, his voice iced, "is a question I cannot answer."

Joan laughed as they gathered their suitcases and started for the waiting room.

"I guess you really got told off, didn't you?" she joked. "That's what you get for sticking your nose into other people's business."

"It didn't hurt to ask."

"No, but you didn't find out anything, did you?"

Miss Duncan swept Mabel Cruse into her arms, and they both cried a little. It was some minutes later before she introduced her old friend to the girls.

"And I should introduce Steve to all of you," Mabel said, laughing pleasantly. "This is Stephen Calverley."

The stocky, brown-haired ten-year-old shook hands with them gravely.

"This has been as sad a day for Steve as it has been happy for us," Mabel explained. "We just put his mother and dad on a plane for the States half an hour ago."

Questions came to the eyes of Miss Duncan and the girls.

"Yes?"

"His mother has been quite ill, and the doctors in Rotterdam haven't been able to find out what was wrong with her. So his dad decided to take her back to their family doctor at home." She put her hand on Steve's shoulder. He frowned up at her and pulled away. "So," she went on, "he's staying with us until they get back."

"That's fine," Joan put in, her smile warm and friendly. "I like boys."

"That," Miss Duncan said dryly, "is the understatement of the year."

Felicia snickered.

Mabel had her car at the airport and drove them through the narrow, twisting streets to the center of Amsterdam, talking with Miss Duncan all the while.

"Would you mind telling me just where we're going?" Joan asked during a brief lull in the conversation.

"To the Bible Boat," Steve answered quickly.

Joan stared down at him.

"Did you say, 'Bible Boat'?"

"That's right," he replied brightly. "That's where we're living. On the Bible Boat, right on the canal."

"Oh, that sounds exciting."

"It would be," he acknowledged, the smile fading from his face, "if there was anybody but *girls* living there."

Joan made a little face at him.

"And what's wrong with girls?" she questioned.

"They don't like to play football or ping-pong or anything. All they want to do is sit around and read and talk and stuff like that."

Joan eyed him impishly.

"If you've got a ping-pong table, I'll take you on."

"You will?" His eyes brightened. "Honest?"

"Right after dinner."

"Oh, boy!" he exclaimed.

When they reached the Bible Boat, Steve got out of the car and struggled with Joan's bags. A Dutch boy his own age, who was not quite as tall or heavy as Steve, came over to help him.

"Here," he said in passable English. "Let me have that one."

Steve jerked it away from him.

"You can take those, Karlje." He motioned to Felicia's luggage with his head. "I'm taking these."

Karlje started to argue with him.

"All those bags are going to be too heavy for you, Steve," Mabel Cruse said quietly. "Why don't you let Karlje have one of them and one of Felicia's?"

"I can carry them all right," the young American muttered. Nevertheless, he did as she suggested.

Felicia smiled her amusement.

"We haven't been here more than two hours, and already you've got boys fighting over you."

"And I'll bet you'd like to have either one of them," Joan laughed.

While the girls went into the Bible Boat with Miss Duncan and Mabel to meet the Dutch half of the missionary team, the boys carried the rest of the luggage inside. They found Joka Vanderende as charming as Mabel had proved to be. She, too, spoke English with only a trace of accent.

"I see you have stolen my boy friends," she teased, winking at Joan and Felicia. "What is it, Stephen and Karlje? Don't you like me anymore?"

Steve blushed delicately.

"Aw–"

"They're Joan's boyfriends," Felicia said. "She stole them by promising to play ping-pong with them."

"But I play ping-pong with you," she countered.

"Sure, Tante Joka," Steve admitted, "but you always beat us."

"They are two fine boys anyway," Joka went on. "And they know I am just teasing them."

Soon Karlje went home, and Steve walked to the corner with him.

"Karlje speaks English very well," Miss Duncan observed. "That must indicate a very superior application in the classroom." She was looking pointedly at Joan.

"Oh, he didn't learn English over here," Joka replied. "He lived in New York with his parents for three and a half years. He went to school there."

Joan looked up at Miss Duncan. A smile stole across her face, danced in her eyes, and lifted the corners of her mouth.

Miss Duncan did not reply, but she colored delicately.

"Karlje has been very good for Steve," the missionary went on. Especially during the time his mother has been sick. Steve has learned a little Dutch, but he and his parents have only been here a year. And that isn't long enough to learn much of the language. I'm afraid Steve would be quite alone while his parents are in America if it weren't for Karlje."

After dinner that evening, Mabel and Joka took their guests on a tour of the boat.

"We talk about the Bible Boat," Mabel said, "but actually there are two boats anchored together. We live in one and have our Bible clubs in the other."

The oldest boat had three bedrooms, a kitchen, small living room, and bath. The newer boat had a small office that doubled as a counseling room, a little kitchen where refreshments could be prepared for the children who came to club, and a large meeting room that could seat fifty comfortably.

"We push the furniture to one side after the meeting or on nights when the kids gather and play ping-pong or games," Mabel explained.

"I see you have put the Wellington philosophy to work here," Miss Duncan said, pride tinging her voice. "Christ in every facet of a girl's life."

They were still looking at the boat when there was a knock at the door.

"Now, who could that be?" Miss Duncan asked.

"It's probably some of the girls who have come to see what to take along to camp tomorrow."

Miss Duncan straightened suddenly.

"Camp tomorrow?" she echoed. "You didn't tell us that you're having camp beginning tomorrow!"

There was a brief silence.

"Joka and I talked it over," Mabel said lamely. "She's going to take care of camp, and I'm going to stay here with you and take care of Stephen."

Miss Duncan shook her head.

"You are going to do no such thing. Camp is one of the most important events of the year for a missionary's work. It's the place where people are saved and children make a dedication of their lives to Christ. You can't leave it and stay here with us, Mabel. It wouldn't be fair to your work."

"I can handle it all right," Joka said. "We have everything worked out."

"But you do *need* Mabel, don't you?"

"Well–" There was a short hesitation.

"Of course, you need her." Miss Duncan's voice rose. "We're going to leave here on the first plane in the morning!"

CHAPTER 2

A WEEK ALONE

You can't do that, Amelia!" Mabel Cruse exclaimed. "It's been years since you and I have had an opportunity to visit. We can't let you leave so soon."

"I'd never forgive myself if I allowed our stay here to interfere with your ministry," Miss Duncan repeated. "Some of those girls might never have another chance to make a decision for Christ if you both aren't at camp with them."

"Couldn't you go to camp with us?" Joka asked.

Miss Duncan turned the suggestion over in her mind.

"I suppose that could be done," she said at last, "but it would be quite a distraction to have both Stephen and the girls along. Since they can't speak Dutch, I don't suppose they could do very much to help with camp."

"I'm afraid not," Mabel answered candidly, "but we'd be glad to have them."

Felicia spoke up thoughtfully. "I was just thinking. Joan and I could stay here with Steve."

"Wouldn't you be afraid to stay alone?"

"Afraid?" Joan echoed. "What's there to be afraid of?"

"Have you forgotten, Mabel?" Miss Duncan asked. "A Wellington girl is taught to fear nothing but fear."

Steve's eyes widened.

"You mean you'll stay here with me?" he asked incredulously. "So I won't have to go to that stupid girls' camp?"

"Is that all right with you?" Joan asked.

"All right with me?" His eyes were dancing. Then he checked himself, and his eyes narrowed. "It'll be okay if I can have Karlje stay with me."

Joan and Felicia looked at the missionaries.

"I think it would be all right," Joka said, "if Amelia and the girls have no objections."

* * *

The following morning, the missionaries and Miss Duncan got on the bus loaded with chattering twelve- to fourteen-year-old girls and headed for camp, sixty-two miles from Amsterdam. They hadn't been gone more than half an hour or so when Karlje came over to the Bible Boat with his clothes in a paper sack.

"Does your mother care if you come to stay with us while Miss Mabel and Tante Joka are gone?" Felicia asked.

He shook his head.

"It gave her room for my Uncle Hans. He came and wanted to stay last night, but we didn't have a bed for him."

"I'm glad it worked out."

The four of them went into the Bible Boat and Karlje put his things away.

For a time, they sat in the living room talking.

"I sure am glad you said you'd stay here with me," Steve told them. "I didn't want to go down to that girls' camp. Imagine, having to spend a whole week in a place where there was nothing but *girls!*"

"Felicia and I are girls," Joan reminded him.

"But you're different," he told them firmly. "You're cool!"

"There's one thing you guys are going to have to do for us tomorrow," Joan said after a while. "You've got to take us shopping."

"Sure we will," Steve said quickly. "We'll take you into all kinds of stores. Just tell us what you want to buy."

"Joan said we wanted to go shopping," Felicia countered, "not *buying*. The chances are that neither of us will have money enough along to buy very much."

Felicia and Joan had a time of Bible reading and prayer with Steve and Karlje before sending the boys to bed. Karlje prayed earnestly for his parents and relatives.

"Dear God, You know all about them," he began, as seriously as though the Lord was bodily in the room with him. "And You know about my Uncle Hans, how he doesn't want to work anymore but just sits around all day trying to paint pictures. Help him to see that he should let God have his life and quit living the way he is and—" It was a long time before Karlje got to the end of his prayer list.

When he finished praying, there were tears in Felicia's eyes.

"What are you crying about?" he asked earnestly.

She shook her head but did not answer him directly.

"Did you ever hear praying like that?" Joan asked when the boys were in their bedroom. "It seemed to me as though Karlje had a private telephone line that led directly to God."

Felicia nodded.

"I'm sure it seemed that way to him too," she said. "He prays as though he knows God is right there listening to him and is just waiting to answer."

The next morning as soon as the stores were open, Steve and Karlje took the girls on their shopping expedition.

"I'd like to get a gift for my Dad," Joan said. "I've been thinking of a small oil painting to hang in his office. Something not too expensive."

Karlje's eyes danced.

"My Uncle Hans paints," he reminded her.

But she could not tell whether he was teasing her or not.

"I think I'd rather look in a store first, if you don't mind."

With Karlje as their guide, they went up one narrow, twisting street and down another. He led them to several small, out-of-the-way art stores, but she could find nothing.

"I didn't know it was so hard to buy a picture," Steve said.

"Neither did I," Joan countered. "I don't know whether it's me or the paintings we've seen." Disappointment crept into her eyes. "But if I find one I like, I can't afford it. And if I find one I can afford, I don't like it."

"I still think you ought to get him some good Dutch leather goods or one of the Delft pieces we've seen," Felicia suggested. "They're both beautiful. I'm sure he'd like them."

Joan's lips pursed thoughtfully.

"They probably would be all right," she said, "but I've had my heart set on getting him an oil painting – if I can find something."

"My Uncle Hans–" Karlje began once more.

"We may have to look at what your Uncle Hans has painted after all," Joan said smiling.

"I don't know if he is so good, but he has a whole room full of pictures."

Joan noted the time.

"We ought to be able to go to one more shop before closing time," she said.

Karlje nodded.

"Is there another art store close by?"

"Not too far," he told her. "Five, six blocks maybe."

Steve sighed deeply but went along without protest. Karlje led the girls across the canal and followed it until he came to a street so narrow a car would have difficulty in driving along it.

Joan stopped and for a moment stared up the street apprehensively. It was late in the afternoon, and the shadows stretched across it, dark with foreboding.

"This way," Karlje said impatiently.

"But it's so dark and–and–" she shivered.

"Come on," Felicia said, taking her by the arm. "This might be just the place that has what you want."

Karlje guided them up the street a block or two, stopping at last before a tiny shop with oil paintings in the window.

"See," he exclaimed triumphantly.

"I didn't think you could do it."

They opened the door and stepped inside. The shopkeeper hadn't yet turned on the lights, and the interior of his store was even darker than the street. The girls looked around with growing uneasiness.

"I think we'd better get out of here," Joan whispered.

As though that was the signal, a door in the rear

opened, and a thin, waspish man came out and greeted them in broken English.

"Good afternoon, ladies," he said.

"You speak English!" Felicia exclaimed.

"Five years I worked at the art museum in New York City," he told them.

Joan was eyeing him curiously. "But how did you know we're Americans?"

He laughed.

"Everybody knows an American." He switched on a light. "You wish to buy something?"

"I'm not really sure," Joan said hesitantly. "I've been trying to find an inexpensive oil painting for my dad to hang in his study."

His smile was broad.

"An oil? That would be nice. Very nice. Do you want a figure? A landscape?"

"I'm not sure. I was just trying to find something I was sure he'd like."

"A portrait of yourself, perhaps?" he suggested. "I can commission a very fine young artist to do your portrait for only five thousand euros."

"Five thousand euros?" she repeated.

"That would be about five thousand American dollars."

Joan gasped.

"It would make your father so happy to have such a masterpiece of you."

"You don't know my father," she replied.

The proprietor followed her to the door.

"Isn't there something else I can show you?" he asked. "A nice watercolor, perhaps? We have some modern masterpieces for only three hundred euros. Some day they will be worth a small fortune."

"Thank you," she said, "but I'm afraid I'll have to leave them for someone else. I can't afford nearly so much."

"I see." His manner froze.

Once outside, she turned to Felicia.

"I'm afraid I'm going to have to find something in leather or Delft after all. I had no idea paintings would cost so much."

"Maybe if you wait until Mabel and Joka get back, they can help you find what you want."

Joan shrugged her shoulders. "Frankly, I'm about to give up."

* * *

The following morning, Steve and Karlje played along the canal, and that afternoon they took Felicia and Joan on a boat ride. It was almost six o'clock in the evening when they finally returned.

"That was a beautiful trip, boys," Felicia said as they went into the houseboat and sat down. "I don't know when I've enjoyed anything so much."

Joan kicked off her shoes and stretched luxuriously.

"Now, if the servants would just fix dinner and serve it to me right here, I'll be completely happy."

"Don't look at me," Felicia reminded her. "I did the cooking yesterday."

Joan got to her feet.

"That's one thing I don't like about you, Felicia," she said, wrinkling her nose at her best friend. "You've got such a good memory." With that she turned to Steve and Karlje. "Come on, guys. I've got some potatoes for you to peel."

"How'd we get in on all of this?" Steve wanted to know.

"The same way I did," Joan said. "You just got drafted."

They had dinner in the kitchen, and Joan played Karlje a game of chess while Steve helped Felicia with the dishes.

"There," he exclaimed, setting the last plate on the counter. "That's done."

"You can hang the towel on that rack by the window."

He started to do so but stopped in his tracks.

"Steve," Joan said, "what's the matter?"

He did not answer her.

"Steve." She raised her voice slightly. "Whatever are you looking at?"

"There's a guy out here watching the boat," he said.

"Why would anyone want to watch the Bible Boat?" Felicia broke in quickly.

"I don't know," he replied, "but he's sure staring in this direction."

"Let me see." Joan stood and started for the window.

"Don't look from there!" Felicia warned. "Go into the other room where it's dark."

"I don't see anyone," Joan called from the bedroom half a minute later.

"He's gone now."

Felicia turned accusingly to Steve. "Are you sure you weren't trying to scare us?"

"Scare you?" His young face was serious. "Why would I try to do that?"

Joan came back into the kitchen.

"Well," she said, "I'm not going to worry about it. I'm going to go to bed."

"That," her blond companion replied, "is a very good idea."

They undressed and silently crawled into bed. It was several minutes before either of them spoke.

"Joan," Felicia said at last. "Joan, are you asleep?"

Her friend rolled over on her side.

"What is it?"

"I was just wondering about something."

"About that guy Steve said he saw?" Joan asked.

Felicia nodded.

"Do you really think he saw someone watching the boat?"

"I'm sure he did," Joan replied. "He's a Christian. And besides, Mabel and Joka both said he's very reliable. I'm sure he wouldn't tell us something that wasn't true."

"Why do you suppose anyone would be watching the boat?" Felicia sighed. In spite of herself, concern tightened the muscles in her throat.

Although it was warm in the room, Joan shivered.

"I don't know," she whispered. "And what's more, I don't want to find out."

CHAPTER 3

STRANGE GUESTS

Felicia tossed restlessly for an hour or so before finally drifting off to sleep. And when she did, she dreamed of grim, dark-faced men who lurked in the shadows and peered intently in the direction of the Bible Boat. When she got up the next morning, however, the thought that somebody may have been watching the Bible Boat seemed ridiculous indeed. She pulled back the curtain and looked out into the brilliant morning sunlight. The murky water of the canal was sparkling.

"Joan, are you going to stay in bed all day?"

Her friend opened her eyes and leaned on one elbow.

"What's bothering you now?" she asked. "Is there another man watching the boat?"

"Nothing like that." Felicia crossed to the closet and removed a shirt from a hanger. "To tell you the truth, I'm beginning to doubt there even was a man who was watching the boat."

"You mean you think Steve was telling us something that wasn't true?" She, too, got out of bed and dressed.

"Not at all," she replied. "But I just noticed that the streetcar goes by the corner. Steve's mysterious stranger could simply have been someone waiting for a car."

"If I'd known that, I could have saved myself from some bad dreams last night," Joan said. "Everywhere I looked, someone was hiding behind a building, a tree, or a bridge watching me. I spent the whole night running." She chuckled. "I was glad to wake up this morning so I could quit dreaming and get a little rest."

They went to the kitchen and started breakfast. Felicia, who was standing at the window, gasped suddenly.

"What is it?" Joan asked, her young voice catching. "Do you see someone out there?"

Felicia shook her head. "No, but I just realized something. Stephen's man couldn't have been waiting for a streetcar. The corner can't be seen from this window."

Something akin to fear flickered in Joan's dark eyes.

"Now why'd you have to tell me that?" she asked in mock indignation. "Why couldn't you let me go on being ignorant – and relaxed?"

Felicia poured the coffee.

"Oh, well," she reasoned. "I suppose it's nothing, really. Why would anyone want to watch the Bible Boat? Neither of us has any money, and there's nothing in here worth stealing."

"It looks as though breakfast's ready," Joan said. "I'd better wake our little friends."

Karlje and Steve were already up and almost dressed.

"We smelled the coffee," Steve said.

"You're too small to drink coffee, Buster."

"Who said anything about drinking it?" he countered. "I just said we smelled it."

"And," Karlje added, "where there's coffee, there's breakfast."

They finished breakfast, and Felicia led their morning devotions.

"Now," Joan said, getting up quickly and starting to stack the dishes. "Let's get the dishes washed and the boat cleaned up so we can go out sightseeing again today."

There was a timid knock at the door, and, automatically, Felicia turned to open it. A boy and girl several years younger than Steve and Karlje stood on the little porch looking up at her seriously.

"Hello."

They spoke to her in Dutch.

"I'm sorry," she said, more to herself than to the apple-cheeked pair before her. "I forgot that you don't speak English."

She moved to one side, smiled as warmly as she could, and motioned them to come in. They did so with some hesitation.

Again, they spoke in Dutch. All Felicia could catch was "Miss Mabel" and "Tante Joka." *They must be asking something about the missionaries,* she reasoned.

"Karlje," she called. "I think I'm going to need you."

He spoke to the youngsters, and a torrent of words rushed out.

"This is Tuenis Voermeer and his sister Wilhelmina," Karlje said. "We call her Wil."

"Good morning, Tuenis." Felicia stooped and held out her hand. "Good morning, Wil."

They both smiled timidly.

"They came over to see Miss Mabel and Tante Joka," Karlje interpreted. "They want to know when Bible club will start again and if they can come when it does."

"Tell them that we know the missionaries would be delighted to have them but that clubs won't start again until after the camps are over."

As he repeated what she said, the smiles left their round faces.

"Look at them," Joan said, tenderness softening her voice. "They're about to cry because they can't go to Bible club."

"It makes a person want to stay here, learn to speak Dutch, and help out, doesn't it?" said Felicia.

Joan nodded.

"They could sure use some more missionaries right here in Amsterdam," she said. "There ought to be someone to keep the clubs going while Mabel and Joka are away at camp."

"And someone to start new clubs. If these kids are so anxious to come, there must be a lot of others who are too."

Sorrowfully, the youngsters turned to leave.

"Ask them to wait a minute, Karlje," Felicia said. "Tell them that if they'd like to stay, I'll fix them something to drink."

Tuenis and Wil smiled shyly and allowed Karlje to usher them back to the table where they sat down in silence. Wide-eyed, they watched Felicia and Joan get ice from the refrigerator, open an envelope of Kool-Aid, and mix it with water and sugar.

"There," Joan exclaimed, setting tall cold glasses of orange drink before them. "And, would they like some cookies, Karlje?"

"They sure would," the young interpreter said quickly, without posing the question to the youthful Dutch visitors.

"Oh, they would, would they?" Joan said. "And just how do you know they would?"

"Because Steve and I would too," Karlje explained, grinning impishly.

"That's a sneaky way of getting some for yourselves," she replied good-naturedly. "That's all I can say."

Before she could get the cookies from the cupboard, there was a loud, imperative knock on the door.

"Sounds as though we've got lots of company this morning," Felicia said.

She turned and would have opened the door, but Karlje reached it first. The instant he released the catch, the door was thrown open and a big, heavyset woman pushed her way into the kitchen. Her round face was flushed crimson, and anger clouded her eyes. She was staring at the children who cringed before her gaze.

"Tuenis!" Her hand closed over the cowering boy's shoulder, and he cried out in pain, struggling to free himself from her grasp. But that was useless. The more he squirmed, the tighter she squeezed.

Wil scooted back from the table, terror flickering in her eyes, and edged toward the door. The big woman directed a torrent of Dutch at the two children, then released Tuenis, who was too frightened to move.

Deliberately, she turned and began to upbraid Felicia and Joan. The young American girls couldn't understand a word she said, but they had no trouble understanding her meaning. Her voice rose to a shout. She shook her finger under their noses and pointed at her children.

"But–But–" Felicia sputtered.

"No speaka the Dutch!" Joan blurted in desperation. "No speaka the Dutch!

Even if the woman could have understood her,

she wouldn't have known what Joan was saying. She wasn't listening. The tirade came to a climax and gradually subsided as the woman's fury spent itself. She shook her fist at the ashen-faced Felicia once more, lashed Joan with a final outburst, and shoved her youngsters out the door ahead of her.

The storm was over. The quiet that enveloped them seemed only to heighten the suspense.

Felicia and her companions stared at the still-open door.

"Whew!" Steve exclaimed. "Was she ever mad!"

"Who was that?" Joan asked of no one in particular.

"And what was that all about?" Felicia wanted to know.

"She was mad because Tuenis and Wil had come here to the boat," Karlje said. He, too, was sallow and shaken. "She said she was going to whip them with a strap if they come over here again."

"She wouldn't do that, would she?" Joan asked incredulously.

"Don't kid yourself," Felicia broke in. "To tell you the truth, I'm glad she didn't have a strap when she was shaking her fist in my face. I'm afraid she'd have used it."

"She said that Miss Mabel and Tante Joka were trying to steal Tuenis and Wil away from her, and she wasn't going to have it! She–" Karlje tried to swallow the lump in his throat. "She said she isn't going to let them come to the boat again. If they do, she's going to go to the police and–and have the missionaries arrested."

A strange look came to Felicia's face. It was a minute or two before she could speak.

"I don't think I've ever heard anything so terrible. All we were doing this morning was giving the children a glass of Kool-Aid and a couple cookies."

"She calls that stealing them," Karlje reminded her.

Joan's eyes snapped.

"People like that shouldn't even have children."

Felicia inhaled deeply. "Well," she said, "I'm glad it's all over."

"If it is," Joan added.

"What do you mean?"

"A woman like that is capable of anything."

Felicia sat down at the table thoughtfully. "We've got to remember," she began, "that in her way, the woman is doing what she thinks is best for her children."

"But to be so bitter against Christianity that she'd threaten to beat them if they come here to the Bible Boat again," Joan said, shuddering. "I can't understand it."

"Neither can I. But it's like a veteran missionary said one time in our church back home. He said that when things like that happen, we've got to remember that it's Christ they hate, not us."

Joan pondered that for a time.

"There's something to that," she observed at last.

They had planned on going sightseeing that day, but for some reason the incident with the irate mother took the heart out of them. Instead they sat around the boat most of the day. Toward evening, they went for a brief walk before returning to the house to fix dinner.

"Don't forget to pray again for Tuenis and Wil before you go to bed," Felicia reminded Karlje and Stephen after they had had their devotions together and had prayed for the youngsters there.

"We will," Karlje promised.

"But I don't know how we're going to be able to do anything about leading them to Christ," Joan went on. "They can't come to the boat any more for Bible club. And even if they could come here, there's nobody but Karlje who could speak to them."

The boys looked at one another. A smile cracked Steve's solemn face.

"Karlje and I have got an idea about what to do about Tuenis and Wil," he said mysteriously.

"What is it?" Joan asked.

"We'll tell you one of these days."

"It isn't something that'll get you in bad with their mother, is it?" Felicia demanded. "She might get so mad at you she'd throw you in the canal."

Steve flinched slightly but that was all. "She can't do anything," he continued. "She isn't going to know anything about it. At least for a while."

"And that," Karlje broke in with finality, "is all we're going to tell you."

Felicia hesitated a moment or two.

"All right," she said, "we won't ask you anything more about this plan of yours, *if* you'll promise to tell us about it before you put it into effect."

The boys looked at one another questioningly.

"Okay?"

"Okay."

Soon they went to bed, and Felicia and Joan could hear their muffled whispering as they got into their pajamas.

"What do you think those boys are going to do?" Joan wondered.

"I don't know," Felicia replied. "Nothing, I hope. If that woman found out they were trying to lead her children to Christ, there's no knowing what she'd do."

They were still talking when there was a hushed knock at the door. Joan abruptly stopped talking. A weak little gasp escaped Felicia's lips.

"Wh-what was that?"

The knock came again.

"There's somebody at the door!"

Felicia noted the time.

"It's after ten thirty," she whispered tautly. "Who'd be coming here at this hour?"

"M-maybe it's the mother of Tuenis and Wil," Joan said numbly.

"That's a happy thought," Felicia shuddered.

CHAPTER 4

SMILING DUTCHMAN

For a minute or two, Felicia and Joan stared at one another, fear glinting silently in their eyes.

The knock came again, louder and more insistent.

"What are we going to do?" Joan whispered between trembling lips.

"We've got to answer it," Felicia said. "If we don't, whoever's there will wake the boys."

She started for the door, but Joan grasped her arm. "Don't open the door, Felicia!" she pleaded.

Felicia managed a crooked little smile. "You don't have to worry about that. I'm no more anxious to have visitors this late at night than you are."

Together they crept out of their bedroom to the kitchen door. The knock came again.

"Wh-who's there?"

"Open the door," a man's voice said in broken English. "I have to talk to you."

"We—we don't want to talk to you," Felicia stammered.

"Open the door," he repeated.

"Whatever you've got to say, you can say from right where you are."

"I have painting to show you. Very valuable painting."

"Painting?" For an instant, Felicia's mind would not track.

"You are the girl who wants to buy painting?"

"Oh," Felicia said. "Oh, he wants to talk to you, Joan."

"I don't want to talk to him," Joan muttered. She raised her voice. "I—I don't think I want to buy a painting anymore."

"If you see this painting, you buy it. This is very good painting. Rembrandt maybe."

"No," Joan said. "I've changed my mind. I don't think I'm going to buy a painting now."

"But you want painting very bad. All over the shops you look. You just *see* this painting, and you want it."

Joan turned to Felicia.

"What're we going to do?" she whispered.

"Keep talking to him. I'll wake Karlje and have him call the police."

Felicia crept stealthily to the boys' room and opened the door. Instantly, they were both awake.

"What's up?" Steve wanted to know, scrubbing

the sleep from his eyes with his fists. "It's not morning, is it?"

"Somebody's trying to break in. We want Karlje to call the police."

Instantly, both boys jumped out of bed.

"Now don't make any more noise than you have to," she cautioned. "Just go in and call the police as quietly as you can and tell them to send somebody over here. A man's trying to get in!"

"Let me in," the voice was saying as Felicia and the boys tiptoed back to the kitchen. "I show you my painting. It is one of the old Dutch masters. I know you want to buy when you see."

"Uncle Hans!" Karlje exclaimed incredulously.

"What?" Joan demanded.

"It is my Uncle Hans," he repeated. He moved forward as though to open the door, but Joan stopped him.

"I don't care if it is your Uncle Hans. We're not letting him in here at this hour."

Karlje raised his voice and began to talk in Dutch. The man outside uttered a few words. Then all was silent.

"He goes now," the boy said. "He won't bother us any more tonight."

Both girls sighed weakly.

"What did you tell him?" Felicia asked at last.

"I just told him that you're afraid to talk to him

at night. He should come back and see you in the daylight."

Joan dropped to a chair, the strength gone suddenly from her body.

"I sure wish we'd known that you told your uncle I was in the market for a picture," she said. "When he knocked on the door, I was so scared I–I almost died."

"Do you think he'll be back tomorrow?" Felicia wanted to know.

Karlje shrugged his shoulders.

After a few minutes, they went back to their bedrooms, but by this time, they were so wide awake that sleep was a long while in coming.

"I wish Karlje had told us he talked with his Uncle Hans about my wanting to buy a picture," Joan said frowning. "If he had, we wouldn't have been frightened at all. I suppose the least we could have done would have been to look at his painting."

Felicia nodded.

"If he wants to sell it badly enough," she replied, "he'll be back."

Joan rolled over and sat up.

"And I'll probably feel so obligated when I do see it that I'll buy it whether I like it or not."

Felicia put her hands beneath her head and stared up at the ceiling.

"I still can't figure out why he didn't come with his painting in the daylight. Why did he wait until dark? And until it was so late there was nobody on the streets?" She pursed her lips thoughtfully. "I don't care if he is Karlje's uncle. There's something strange about all this."

The next morning, Steve and Karlje got up an hour earlier than usual.

"Just what are you two doing up so early?" Joan asked them.

They grinned mysteriously at her.

"Wouldn't you like to know?"

She set their breakfast before them. "As a matter of fact," she said, "I would."

Steve snickered.

They ate their breakfast hurriedly and raced out, slamming the door behind them.

"I wish I knew what those two characters are up to," Joan said, tugging at the lobe of her ear.

"What makes you so suspicious all of a sudden?"

Joan smiled impulsively. "Well, if you want the truth," she said, "I keep thinking of the things I used to do when I was a kid. It's enough to make anyone suspicious."

The girls cleaned the boat thoroughly and sat down to write a few postcards.

Several times during the morning, the boys came back to the boat.

"We'd like to get a hammer," Steve said. "I think there's one in that little drawer near the sink."

Felicia got it for him.

In half an hour, they were back for a saw. Steve got

it from Felicia while Karlje went over to Joan and held out a small parcel wrapped in heavy brown paper.

"I met my Uncle Hans," he explained. "He asked me to bring this painting over to see if you like it."

She unwrapped it slowly and held it up.

"Felicia!" she exclaimed. "It's beautiful!"

"Let me see it." Felicia came over and stood beside her. The painting was a portrait of a very old Dutchman. His face was deeply lined. But he had a gentle smile, and laughter danced in his eyes.

"He looks as though he could speak," Joan said.

"Do you like it?" Karlje asked seriously.

"Like it?" she echoed. "It's beautiful. But I probably couldn't afford it anyway."

"Uncle Hans said if you like it, he'll sell it to you cheap."

"That depends on what he calls cheap," Joan said. "The man in the art store said it would be cheap to have my portrait painted, and he wanted five thousand dollars."

"Uncle Hans said he'd sell it for thirty euros if you like it."

"Thirty euros?" she said in amazement.

"Is that too much?"

"No, it's not too much. Not at all." She studied the painting once more. "I can hardly believe it's so cheap, that's all."

"You give the money to me tonight," Karlje said. "I'll take it to him."

He started for the door.

"You can have it now if you want it."

"Steve and I are too busy," he said. "I'll take it to him tonight."

When he was gone, Joan turned her attention to the painting once more.

"I can hardly believe it's possible to get a painting like this at such a cheap price. I know Dad's going to love it."

The corners of Felicia's mouth pulled to a frown as she looked at the portrait.

"Maybe it's too beautiful," she murmured.

"What do you mean by that?"

"I was just thinking that there might be something wrong with it. That's all."

"I don't see how there could be. Karlje said his uncle is a painter," Joan protested. "He must have painted it himself."

"That still doesn't explain why he didn't come to us himself in the daytime. Or why he didn't sign his name to it. In fact, there's no signature on it that I can see."

Concern dulled the excitement in Joan's eyes.

"Do you suppose it could be a stolen painting?"

"That's what I've been wondering."

"But if it's stolen, why would he want to sell it to us so cheaply?" Joan asked. "At thirty euros, he wouldn't get enough to even bother with."

There was a brief silence.

"That's something I can't figure out," Felicia said uneasily. "Maybe it got too hot for him to keep it." She took a deep breath. "But if that were the reason, he surely wouldn't sell it to us. It could be traced right to him through Karlje."

"Maybe we ought to go and see Karlje's Uncle Hans," Joan said, "and ask him some questions. If we get the right answers, I can pay him the thirty euros and keep the painting. If we're still suspicious, we can make him take it back."

Felicia nodded.

"I think you'd feel better about it if you did. And you might avoid a lot of trouble for yourself."

Joan studied the painting wistfully.

"I can't help hoping that everything is all right," she said quietly. "The more I look at it, the more eager I am to get it."

When Steve and Karlje came back to the Bible Boat that evening, they were tired, dirty, and uncommunicative.

"How'd things go for you two today?" Felicia asked at the dinner table.

"All right, I guess."

"Did you finish what you started?"

They eyed her quickly.

"How'd you find out?" Steve asked.

"About what?"

"You know. About what we're doing?"

Felicia looked curiously at him.

"Why?"

For an instant, he studied her face.

"Oh, skip it."

Karlje grinned impishly at her. "Thought you were going to find out something, didn't you?"

* * *

Without waiting to do the dishes after dinner that evening, they went over to Karlje's to find his Uncle Hans. Uncle Hans lived with Karlje's parents in a third-floor walk-up apartment on a dark, narrow side street.

Although neither of his parents could speak English well, they welcomed the girls and Steve as though they had known them all their lives. Karlje asked about his uncle, but his mother shook her head and replied in a burst of Dutch.

"She says she hasn't seen him since this morning," Karlje explained in English. "She doesn't know where he is but thinks maybe he's in jail again."

"In jail?" Joan's eyes widened. "Has he ever been in jail?"

"Lots of times."

The two girls stared at each other.

"I'm glad you suggested I check into things before I bought the painting," Joan whispered.

In a moment or two, they excused themselves and left the small Dutch apartment.

"I think I ought to go to the police and tell them about the painting, don't you, Felicia?" questioned Joan.

"We could wait until morning," Felicia replied.

"I'd feel better if we went tonight." Joan turned to the boys. "Is it far to the nearest police station?"

"Not very," Steve answered.

"But they won't let you see Uncle Hans," Karlje protested. "Only on visiting days can you see him."

"We aren't going there to see him," Joan explained. "At least not tonight. I just want to go and tell them about the painting, so they'll know we're not trying to keep anything from them."

Karlje and Steve guided the girls to the nearest police station several blocks from the Bible Boat, and they all went inside. The officer at the desk was busy with a sheaf of papers.

"We—we'd like to talk to someone," Karlje said hesitantly in Dutch.

The man at the desk did not look up.

"It—it's about a painting."

"Can't you see I'm busy? Go away and quit bothering me."

"But—but it's very important."

Impatiently, the police officer pushed the papers aside and raised his head.

"What do you want?"

"These American ladies have a painting they

want to talk to you about. They are afraid it might be stolen."

"I see." Momentarily, he drummed on the desk with his pencil. "There is no one here who can speak English tonight. Ask them if they could leave the painting with me and come back tomorrow."

The boy repeated his request to Joan.

"But the painting isn't here," she protested. "It's at the boat."

"If they will come back tomorrow morning at ten o'clock," the officer said, "there'll be someone here to talk to them. And have them bring the painting with them."

For a minute or two, Joan remained motionless before the police desk, but the officer on duty had already turned back to his papers as though they weren't even in the room.

"We'd just as well go," Karlje said softly.

"I–I suppose so," Joan replied. "It doesn't look as though we're going to be able to accomplish anything else here tonight."

They turned and went out into the chilly, damp night.

"He certainly didn't seem to be very interested," Joan went on as they walked along the street in the direction of the canal. "He acted as though he didn't care whether the painting had been stolen or not."

"I'm sure he is," Felicia said. "He acted to me as

though he was embarrassed that he couldn't speak English to us."

"At any rate, he knows I was in and tried to tell him about it," Joan said, shrugging her shoulders. "If they find out Karlje's Uncle Hans lifted it from some place, they won't be able to throw me in the clink for it."

Steve, who had been walking along in silence, tugged suddenly at the sleeve of Felicia's sweater.

"Felicia," he whispered in guarded tones.

She looked down.

"What is it, Steve?"

"Somebody's following us."

She gasped audibly.

"There're two of them about half a block behind us. They were waiting across the street when we came out of the police station!"

CHAPTER 5

THE CHASE

Joan would have looked back, but Felicia stopped her instantly.

"Don't do that," she warned under her breath. "We don't want them to know we've noticed them following us."

"If they are following us," Joan countered. "They could just happen to be going our way – I hope."

"They're following us all right," Karlje put in.

"Just what makes you so sure?" Joan asked. Nevertheless, she quickened her pace.

"Let's go across the street," Steve said. "If they cross over, we'll *know* they're after us."

"Oh no!" she protested. "It's darker over there th-th-than it is here. We don't want to make it any easier for them to–to grab us than it is already."

"We can cross the street at the next corner," Felicia said.

"If we have to, we have to," Joan said in mock resignation. "Do you suppose they'll put it in the papers tomorrow so our parents'll find out what's happened to us?"

"Joan!" Felicia scolded. "Don't talk that way! You said yourself that we don't even know if they're actually following us or not."

At the corner, they crossed to the other side of the street. It was darker there. The streetlights were fewer, and the awnings over the store fronts seemed to create a long black void for them to walk through.

"Brrr," Joan managed between clenched teeth.

Steve looked back.

"Those guys are crossing the street too!" he whispered tautly.

By this time, Felicia and her companions were almost running. They crossed the next street and hurried up another long, dark block. Every now and then, one or the other of the boys looked back.

"They're gaining on us!" Karlje gasped in sudden desperation.

"Come on!" Felicia cried.

Taking hold of Steve's hand, she burst into a run. Joan grasped Karlje's small brown arm and did the same. Faster and faster, they sped along the deserted walk.

"This way!" Karlje ordered, approaching the street that led to the canal and the Bible Boat.

They rounded the corner and raced for the canal.

The men behind them were drawing closer and closer. They could hear the sound of their feet running on the walk behind them. Felicia stumbled and would have fallen if Steve hadn't held tightly to her hand.

Joan and Karlje were several paces ahead by the time she regained her balance.

"Hurry!" Steve shouted. "We're almost there!"

Joan reached the Bible Boat first. Fingers trembling, she jerked the key from her purse and thrust it hurriedly into the lock. There was a welcoming click of metal, and the door opened. The men were only a few paces behind them as they crowded inside and slammed the door shut. Joan flicked the lock and threw the guard chain into place. Then, turning slowly, she allowed a long, deep sigh to escape her lips.

For a brief moment, nobody spoke or moved. They just stood there, faces ashen and chests heaving as they fought to breathe.

"Whew!" Joan exclaimed when she could talk again. "I never thought we'd make it!"

"Neither did I!" Felicia agreed. She was still weak and trembling. "Every step we took I thought would be our last. And when I almost fell!" An icy shudder ran up her spine. "If it hadn't been for Steve, I don't know what would have happened to me."

"All I could think about was getting back here to the boat before they grabbed us and threw us into the canal!" exclaimed Steve.

"We're here safely now," Felicia replied. "That's all that matters."

Joan jerked erect.

"If it is really over and we're safe from them," she said, her taut voice hesitant and uncertain.

"What do you mean by that?" Felicia demanded.

"How do we know those guys aren't out there somewhere waiting until we think it's all clear b-b-before they break in and—and get us?"

"Now why did you have to bring that up?" Steve asked.

"Maybe it was just my Uncle Hans wanting to talk to you about getting paid for his painting," Karlje suggested. "Did you ever think of that?"

"If that was your Uncle Hans, I'd like to talk to him for a couple of minutes right now," Joan said firmly. "I'd tell him a thing or two, scaring us this way."

Karlje crossed the kitchen and fumbled for the light switch.

"I guess we'd just as well turn on the lights so we can see what we're doing and—"

"Don't do that!" Felicia cried, leaping toward him. "As long as there's a chance those m-m-men are out there, we're not going to turn on the lights to let them know where we are in the boat and what we're doing."

"We could pull down the blinds."

"No lights," she repeated sternly.

In the dim half-light from the floods that illumined

the bridge fifty yards away, they stared at one another questioningly.

"What should we do?" Joan asked.

Felicia thought for a moment.

"We could call the police," she suggested, "but we wouldn't have anything concrete to tell them."

"You mean it would be better to wait until they break in?" Joan asked. "I can't say that I agree with you."

'What I was really thinking," Felicia went on, "is that we ought to have Karlje close to the phone so he can call the police if those men do approach the boat. I'm sure they could get here before anything could happen."

"You mean you *hope* they could get here in time."

Steve moved cautiously to the window and peered out.

"See anything?" Karlje asked. He would have joined his American friend, but Joan spoke up.

"Karlje! You're getting away from the phone."

"But–"

"Come over here and sit down." She located a chair in the dark and moved it near the table. "Now you sit here and hold the phone on your lap – like this."

"But–"

"And be sure and have your hand on the telephone. Is that clear?"

"But–"

"You sound like a balky motorbike, saying 'but' all the time. What're you sputtering about?"

"But I don't know the telephone number."

Joan gasped.

"Oh, my goodness! Where's the paper with the important numbers on it? Felicia, what did you do with it?"

She caught her toe on the leg of Karlje's chair and sprawled flat. The boys both snickered.

Joan rolled over and sat up.

"You guys would laugh at me!" she exploded good-naturedly. "Just for that, I have a notion to put you outside and let those men have you."

"Here's the paper," Felicia said, laughing in spite of herself.

She handed it to Karlje.

"I can't read it without some light," he protested.

"Here." Joan felt around until she located a box of matches in the cupboard. Striking one, she held it for him until he found the number and repeated it carefully. "Now, do you think you can remember it?"

"I can try."

"I'll memorize it, too," she promised. "But I know that if th-th-those guys do try anything, I–I'll be so s-s-scared, I'll forget it."

Once the matter of the phone and the police number was settled, silence fell over the little group. Felicia and Joan sat at the kitchen table, and Karlje was on a chair nearby with the phone on his lap.

Steve remained at the window, pulling back the shade slightly and peering out.

"See anything?" Karlje asked him after a time.

He shook his head. "No. Not now."

"What do you mean, 'not now'?" Joan asked quickly.

"There were a couple of guys out there a few minutes after we got in here and locked the door," Steve said. "They walked back and forth, talking to each other and looking over this way every once in a while. But after a few minutes they walked away and haven't been back since."

"Well, that's a relief. I, for one, am not going to miss them very much."

"If they're really gone," Felicia cautioned. "They just might do something like that to make us think they've given up, so we'll let down our guard a little."

Joan turned to her.

"I don't know why I even run around with you," she teased. "You always have to spoil everything. I just about had myself talked into the notion that it was safe for us to go to bed and go to sleep, and you have to come up with a remark like that."

Nobody else replied, and the minutes passed endlessly. Steve turned from the window after a time and, yawning, found his way through the darkness to an easy chair in the other room. Karlje nodded sleepily, and, at last, his limp hand slipped from the telephone on his lap.

"Look at him, Felicia," Joan said, smiling. "He finally fell asleep."

"I've been about to do the same thing myself for the last half hour."

"I don't think there's any danger of those guys coming back now and trying to get in, do you?"

Felicia shook her head.

"If they were going to do it, I think they'd have tried a long time ago."

They wakened the dozing boys and sent them into their bedroom.

"This doesn't seem real somehow," Joan said as she and her friend crawled into bed. "It's more like a bad dream."

"It just doesn't add up," Felicia murmured. "I can't figure it out at all."

"While you're trying, I'm going to get a little sleep," Joan told her.

CHAPTER 6

VISIT FROM TWO REPAIRMEN

The next morning, Steve and Karlje were up as early as though nothing had happened the night before. Felicia heard them stirring and shook her sleeping friend.

"It's time to get up, Joan."

Joan groaned.

"Joan, we've got to get up."

Protesting, she turned over and sighed deeply.

"Know something, Felicia?" she said. "You've been around Miss Duncan so much you're getting more like her every day."

When Felicia went into the kitchen a few minutes later, Steve and Karlje were rummaging through the drawers in the cupboard.

"Looking for something special?" she asked.

"Nails." Steve didn't even look up. "We ran out of them yesterday."

"Well, I don't think you'll find any in the drawer with the silver." Felicia went to a small closet near the door. "How about these? Will they do?"

He picked up one of the nails and looked at it.

"I don't know. Think it's big enough, Karlje?"

The other boy frowned.

"Some bigger nails would be better if we can get them. We'd have to use an awful lot of these."

"How about the ones in this box?" Felicia handed him a small cardboard carton she had found in the bottom of the closet. "Are they big enough for this project of yours?"

"They're just right." Steve beamed. "They're great."

"And what're you doing with nails?" she asked curiously.

An impish grin twisted his bronzed face.

"You'll find out."

"You mean you aren't going to tell me after all the help I've given you?" she implored teasingly.

He hesitated.

"Don't do it," Joan broke in. "You wouldn't tell me yesterday. Make her wait to find out too."

"Oh, I wasn't going to tell her," Steve replied. "I was just trying to figure how to say no without hurting her feelings."

At the breakfast table, they talked about the visit Joan was to make to the police station at ten o'clock that morning.

"I won't have to go along, will I?" Karlje asked.

"I'd sort of thought you'd be going with us," she answered, "but I don't think it would be necessary, do you, Felicia?"

Felicia shook her head.

"The man said someone will be there who speaks English. I don't think we'll really need Karlje."

His young face lit up.

"Oh boy, Steve! Now we won't have to quit work this morning."

As they got ready to leave, Felicia called Steve and Karlje back.

"We'll probably be gone all morning," she said. "Are you guys going to want to get into the boat before noon?"

Steve pursed his lips and glanced at his companion.

"I don't know. We might need something pretty bad. Not being able to get in might delay us for a couple of hours. It might keep us from having this fixed up today."

"If we give you one of our keys, do you think you could hang onto it and not drop it in the canal?" Felicia continued.

"For cryin' out loud," Steve exploded. "What do you think we are? Little kids? Sure we can hang onto a key."

"And can you remember to keep the door locked all the time?" Joan broke in. "We don't want to come home and find one of the guys who chased us last night in the closet or under the bed."

"Sure thing," Steve continued. "We'll lock it when we're not here, and we'll be sure to keep the key."

Felicia went to the sideboard, took out a door key, and gave it to Steve. He put it carefully in his pocket and hurried outside after Karlje.

"I'd like to know what those young scamps are up to," Joan said.

"So would I."

Felicia noticed that the picture of Christ on the wall above the sideboard was crooked. She went to straighten it and broke the string that held it up.

"Now you've done it," Joan said amiably. "That's what comes from being so picky about things. Always leave things alone is my motto. Then you don't have anything to fix."

"Miss Duncan would say you don't have the true Wellington spirit. Wellington girls are supposed to be capable, resourceful, and useful."

"That's exactly what I've been trying to tell you. You sound more like her every day."

"Be quiet, Joan, and get me another piece of string or wire, will you? I think there's something in that drawer behind you."

A moment later Joan held up a short length of copper wire.

"How about this?" she asked. "Will it do?"

Felicia took it without comment. In a minute or two she had the picture on the wall again.

"There," she said. "That ought to hold it."

Joan noted the time.

"We'd better get a move on if we're going to get down to that police station by ten o'clock. It's after nine thirty now."

When they got to the station, the officer at the desk took one look at them, motioned for them to be seated, and disappeared into an inner office. In a couple of minutes, he was back with a superior who greeted them in English.

"I'm sorry we had to ask you young ladies to come back this morning," he said. "If you will please come into my office, I'm sure this won't take long."

The officer was an easy person to talk to. He listened politely as Joan told him about wanting to take an oil painting to her father but not being able to find one she could afford in the shops. She related that Karlje had mentioned it to his Uncle Hans.

"I was crazy about the picture he sent to the Bible Boat with Karlje," she concluded. "But the price was so low we thought we'd better talk with him about it before I bought it. So we went over to Karlje's home, but his Uncle Hans hadn't been there all day, even though he was supposed to meet us there so I could pay him." Joan took a deep breath. "So, we thought we'd better come down and see you. We were afraid the picture had been stolen."

The man behind the big desk tugged thoughtfully at the lobe of his ear.

"We checked our records this morning in

preparation for your visit," he said. "But we have no report of a stolen painting of any kind."

She sighed deeply.

"That's good news."

"Of course, there's a possibility that it could have been stolen and not missed yet or that the owner decided not to report it as stolen for some reason."

The girls looked at one another questioningly.

"Tell me," he continued, "do you have the painting with you?"

Silently, she handed it to him. He unwrapped it with care and held it so the sunlight from the window shone on it.

"Hmmmm," he murmured. "Not bad. Not bad at all."

"The first night he talked to me about it," Joan said, "the night he came to the boat and scared us all half to death, he said he had an 'old master' to sell me. I guess that's another thing that made us suspicious."

It was almost as though he had not heard her. He handed the picture back to her without comment, made a note on the sheet of paper before him, and looked up.

"I'm going to release the painting to you, Miss Bailey," he said. "I see no reason for holding it. I do want to thank you for coming in however. I can well understand why the circumstances would cause you to be suspicious."

He went through the outer office and walked to the door with them.

"And thank you," he said again. "We appreciate your concern and your wish to be completely honest."

The girls walked half a block or so from the station without saying anything.

"Well," Joan said at last, shifting the small brown package from one arm to the other. "I guess that's that. I can send the money home with Karlje and mail the painting to Dad."

But Felicia still was not entirely satisfied.

"I suppose he handles enough of this sort of thing so he knows whether an incident needs looking into further," she began. "But I'm still bothered by all the things that have happened. We don't know why Uncle Hans came to us at night and wouldn't see us during the day. We don't know why he wasn't at Karlje's apartment last night after he was to meet us there. And we don't know why those two men followed us home from the police station. As far as I'm concerned, there are a lot of questions I'd like to have answered."

Joan glanced at her companion.

"Just about the time I start breathing easily, you remind me of some things that get me all upset again."

"Don't pay any attention to me," Felicia countered, laughing. "I'm probably making too much of everything."

By this time, they had once more reached the

Bible Boat. Joan was fumbling for her key when Steve came hurrying up.

"Go on in," he said. "It's unlocked."

"Unlocked?" Felicia repeated, staring at him. "Didn't we ask you to keep it locked while we were gone?"

"Sure you did," he explained. "And we did keep it locked until the guys from the telephone company came. I was just running over now to see if they'd finished so I could lock it again."

They went into the boat and looked around uneasily.

"Men from the telephone company," Joan repeated. "What were they doing here?"

"They came to fix the phone. It was a good thing you left the key with us. If you hadn't, our phone wouldn't have been repaired." He stopped suddenly as he read the concern in their eyes. "Did I do something wrong?"

"No," Felicia told him. "I'd probably have done the same thing."

Steve sighed his relief.

"Karlje and I didn't know what to do," he continued. "We were going to make them wait and come back later, but then we got to thinking about those–those guys who followed us home and we knew you–you'd have to have a telephone tonight, so we opened the door for them."

The girls looked everything over carefully.

"Nothing seems to have been touched," Joan said at last.

Felicia turned to the boy at their side.

"Are you *sure* they were from the telephone company?"

"That's what they *said*."

"Did you see a truck or anything like that?"

He shook his head.

"We didn't even think to look for a truck. There were two of them carrying these tool kits right in broad daylight. We figured they just *had* to be what they said they were."

Felicia was standing in the middle of the kitchen.

"Everything seems to be all right," she said slowly, "but–"

"But what?"

"Didn't I straighten that picture just before we left?" she asked.

"Straighten it?" Joan said, laughing. "You broke the string and had to rehang it. Almost made us late for our appointment with the police."

"That's what I thought." She went over and straightened the picture once more. As she did so her finger touched the stiff wire. Curiously she took the picture from the wall and turned it over. "Joan!" she cried. "This isn't the wire I put on this picture this morning!"

Her friend pressed close to her and stared at the

stiff piece of black wire that was now on the back of the picture.

"Maybe it fell down again," she said lamely.

Felicia shook her head.

"The wire wouldn't have broken," she said, "and it was soft enough to knot easily. I know my knots didn't pull out. Besides, the picture only weighs a few ounces. That wire was taken off by someone."

She looked up at Steve.

"You boys didn't do it, did you?"

He shook his head. "We haven't even been back in the boat since you left except to let those guys in and show them where the phone was."

Joan's face was ashen, and the light in her eyes was gone.

"Why would anyone take a wire from a picture frame?" she asked woodenly. "That's the most stupid thing to steal that I ever heard of."

Felicia went over to another picture.

"Look," she said in a moment or two, her voice lowering to a whisper. "This picture has the same kind of wire on it. And see where it's been cut with pliers. It's new and shiny. Joan, both of these wires were put on these pictures this morning."

"But why?"

"I don't know why." Slowly she drew in a deep breath. "But I'm beginning to doubt that the men Steve and Karlje let in here were from the phone company."

The boy's eyes opened wide.

"Wh-wh-who do you think they were?" he stammered.

She did not answer him.

"Steve," she said hurriedly, "go and get Karlje. Tell him we want him to come back to the boat just as fast as he can."

In five minutes, the two boys were back, panting heavily from having run all the way.

"What is it?" Karlje gasped. "What do you want?"

"As soon as you get your breath, we'd like to have you call the telephone company," Felicia told him. "Find out if they actually sent repairmen here this morning."

The boy did as he was asked. He talked briefly on the phone but held it in his hand for a moment before hanging up.

"What did they say?" Joan demanded.

"They said they didn't have a report that there had been anything wrong with the phone on the boat. The last repair crew was sent here more than a year ago."

Felicia and Joan stared numbly at one another.

"Well," Joan exclaimed. "What do you make of that?"

CHAPTER 7

WORTH OF THE DUTCHMAN

Weakly, Felicia sought a chair and dropped into it. Her hands were trembling slightly, and perspiration beaded her attractive face.

"That can't be right," Joan protested. "Nobody would steal a little piece of wire from the back of a picture. And if he did, why would he take the time to replace it?"

The young blond girl was slow in answering.

"I know it doesn't make sense to you," she said. "It doesn't make sense to me either. Nothing that's happened since Miss Duncan and the missionaries left adds up. But, Joan, we can't get away from the fact that two men wanted to get in here badly enough to pose as telephone repairmen. And when they got in, apparently all they did was remove the wires from a couple of pictures and replace them with new wire."

"And it isn't sensible."

"It doesn't look sensible to us." Her voice lowered to a whisper. "But, Joan, there's a good reason for everything that's happened. All we've got to do is to find it."

The boys were squirming uneasily in their chairs. Finally, Karlje spoke up.

"Are you through with us?"

Felicia smiled and nodded. "I think so. Thanks for making the phone call for us."

They rose to leave.

"I–I'm sorry we let those guys in and caused all the trouble," Steve said.

"You needn't be. There was nothing taken."

He flashed her a quick smile.

"Good. We'll have something to show you tonight maybe." With that he was gone. Karlje was close on his heels.

There was a great deal more sightseeing both girls wanted to do in Amsterdam. They planned to go to the port and see the ocean liners that stop there from all over the world and to visit the palace where the royal family lives. They wanted to take a trip to the north of the country to two little villages where the people still wore their colorful old costumes with wooden shoes and exquisite lace hats. But neither of them felt like it. Instead, they remained inside the Bible Boat all afternoon, talking in low tones if at all.

Late in the afternoon, Joan got out her painting and looked at it once more.

"You know, Felicia," she said thoughtfully, "I've got an idea this painting is at the bottom of this entire business in some way."

The corners of Felicia's mouth tightened to draw her lips to a thin, hard line.

"I'd never thought of that." She picked it up and turned it carefully in her hands. "I suppose it could be. Actually, that's the only logical conclusion."

"Which probably means that it isn't true," Joan said. "Nothing else in this whole affair is logical."

Felicia handed the painting back to Joan.

"Maybe you'd better send it to your dad quick before something else happens."

Joan grinned infectiously. "As a matter of fact, I was thinking of sending it in a day or two, but for a little different reason. If I mail it now, he'll have it for his birthday."

A few minutes later Karlje and Steve came into the boat, grinning broadly.

"Well," Steve announced, "we're ready to show you."

"That's right," Karlje added. "You're the first ones we're taking to see it. That's because you loaned us the hammer and saw and nails and stuff."

"Should we blindfold them till we get there, Karlje?" Steve asked.

"I don't think we'd better. They might fall in the canal."

"That's real thoughtful of you not to want us to fall in the canal," Joan said, her eyes dancing. "Or did you mean we'd be so surprised when you took our blindfolds off that we'd fall in?"

"You just wait. You'll see."

"You've got us so excited we can hardly wait," Felicia said. "Let me get my sweater."

They locked the Bible Boat carefully and allowed the boys to take them first along the canal for a block and a half and then up a side street. As soon as they reached the corner, Steve and Karlje stopped and looked up at the girls.

"Well, what do you think of it?" Karlje asked. Pride tinged his voice.

Halfway up the block was a peculiar wooden structure made of crating and old lumber that extended over the sidewalk.

Neither girl spoke for a minute or two.

"What do you think of it?" Steve asked.

"It's nice." Felicia faltered. "It's very nice. But–"

It was Joan who blurted out the question. "Just exactly what are we supposed to be looking at?" she asked.

"It's our new clubhouse for Bible club," Karlje explained.

"Clubhouse?" Felicia could scarcely believe what she heard.

"Yes, our clubhouse. Tuenis's mom said he and Wil couldn't come to the boat for club anymore, so we fixed a place where they could come," Steve explained.

"It's only big enough for about four of us at a time," Karlje explained, "but if we have more than that, we'll just have to have another meeting."

Felicia shook her head wonderingly.

"Do you mean to tell us that you two boys built this just so Tuenis and Wil would have a place to hear the gospel?"

"Oh, we figure on getting some others to come besides Tuenis and Wil," Steve answered.

"Who's going to take charge?" Joan broke in.

"Well," Karlje replied seriously. "I'm going to lead the singing and the prayer. Steve doesn't know enough Dutch to teach the lesson, so I'm going to interpret for him."

There were tears in Felicia's eyes as she and Joan approached the crude structure with the boys.

"It makes me so ashamed of myself," she said softly, "for the way I've been about witnessing to anyone. This is wonderful."

"We could've done a better job if we'd had more boards," Karlje explained. "We got most of them from my Uncle Hans. That was when he told me about the painting he had and asked me to try to sell it to you for him. He said if I'd do that, he'd give me all the wood we needed. He even loaned us his wheelbarrow so we could haul it over here."

"That was very nice of him," Felicia murmured. Her throat was still dry and constricted.

"I sure wish you two spoke Dutch," Karlje said,

changing the subject suddenly. "If you did, you could teach the lessons for us sometimes."

"We'd like that," Joan said seriously.

"Hey, wait a minute!" Steve exclaimed. "Why couldn't you interpret for them too?"

"That is an idea!" The boys began to plan excitedly for the club meetings they would begin to hold the following day.

While they were talking, Felicia and Joan examined the makeshift lean-to.

* * *

That evening Karlje and Steve worked diligently on their Bible lesson. They made pictures and went over the story repeatedly until they knew it practically word for word.

"I've been thinking I ought to have an expert check this painting before I send it to Dad," Joan said, "just in case it is valuable. But I can hardly ask Steve and Karlje to go with us when they're planning to spend tomorrow holding Bible clubs for the kids in the neighborhood."

"The man in the last place we went spoke English," Felicia said. "We could take it back to him."

"Or," Joan continued thoughtfully, "we could go to a place near one of the big hotels that cater to Americans. They'd surely have somebody who speaks English working there."

The next morning after having prayer for the club meetings Karlje and Steve planned to hold that day, the boys gathered their lesson and materials and left the Bible Boat excitedly.

"I'm beginning to feel as though I'm a bit crazy about this painting," Joan said, wrapping the picture in heavy brown paper once more. "But I'll feel better when I've checked it out with an expert and get it mailed."

"I'll be glad when it's gone too," Felicia said. "Then maybe strange things will stop happening around here."

By this time, the girls knew their way around the center of Amsterdam quite well and had no difficulty in finding an art critic who spoke English. Joan told him about the painting and asked for an appraisal.

"You have the painting along?" he asked, his English as clipped and prim as his wisp of a moustache.

"It's right here." Joan handed him the paper wrapped package.

"Of course," he said, removing the paper with some distaste, "we might not be able to give you an answer immediately. A very bad painting, yes. We can tell at a glance. A good painting, maybe. It takes time to study, perhaps, to determine the depth of originality, the use of color, the portrayal of emotion. But we should be able to give you an approximation of its value quite quickly. On the other hand, if we should suspect it of being a masterpiece!" His eyes widened expressively. "It might take months of painstaking examination by experts to–" He checked himself as he removed the paper and looked at the small oil painting.

For the space of a moment or two, he held it at arm's length studying it. As he did so, the frown lines on his forehead deepened.

"Well?" Joan asked, his very manner causing her own excitement to build.

"Well, what?" he asked coldly.

"What do you think of it?"

"It is not bad. Not bad at all." He looked at it again. "I will say the artist shows some degree of promise if he gets further study and works very hard. In my considered opinion, he could not become a great artist but a good painter – yes, I think I could go that far."

Joan relaxed visibly.

"What would you say the painting's worth?" she asked.

He shrugged his shoulders.

"That is hard to say. To me, it is valueless. To someone who has a personal interest in it – who knows the artist perhaps – it would be worth whatever he would be willing to pay for it."

"Would it be worth thirty euros?" Felicia asked.

"Thirty euros?" He frowned again. "The frame is worth six or seven euros. And there is the canvas. It is small, but it cost something. Yes, I suppose you could say the painting is worth about that. Perhaps we should put it another way. At thirty euros, you would not have been overcharged very much."

Joan rewrapped her painting, thanked him, and she and Felicia left the store.

"Well," Felicia said, "at least you know now what it's worth – and how good you are at judging art."

Joan laughed pleasantly.

"You don't know how relieved I am just to know that I paid all that painting is worth."

"Now we can go back to the boat, wrap it, and mail it with a clear conscience," Felicia said.

On the Bible Boat that afternoon, Joan got some stout cord and was about to wrap the painting when she stopped suddenly.

"I just realized something," she said. "I'm going to have to send this airmail if he's going to get it before his birthday."

"I guess you are at that."

"If I send the frame and all airmail, it's going to cost a small fortune." She pulled out the cutlery drawer, took out an old case knife, and began to pry on the corners of the frame to loosen it. "I'll just send him the painting. I can take the frame home with me when we go."

"Here, let me help you."

Together they removed the painting from the frame.

"Uncle Hans must be hard up," Felicia said. "This piece of cardboard backing was cut out of something else. It's got the floor plan of an apartment and a lot of addresses on it."

"And look what the picture is painted on," Joan continued. "A cheap piece of cloth stiffened with paint and stretched on a frame." She paused momentarily. "Maybe it's like Karlje says. His Uncle Hans has been in jail lots of times. But you can't help feeling sorry for a guy who can't even buy proper materials and has to use things like these for his work."

"We're going to have to hurry, or we're not going to be able to mail it today," Felicia reminded her.

Joan finished wrapping the package, and they went to the post office to mail it. When they returned an hour or so later, a big woman got up from a nearby bench and came toward them.

"Joan!" Felicia whispered under her breath. "Do you know who that is? It's Tuenis and Wil's mother!"

CHAPTER 8

NEWSSTAND ENCOUNTER

Numbly, Felicia and Joan waited for the scowling woman to come up to them.

"Hello," Joan stammered.

"I want to talk to you," she said slowly in English.

"Of course." Felicia managed the best smile she could produce under the circumstances. "Come on in."

Joan unlocked the door to the Bible Boat, and the three of them went into the kitchen and sat down around the table.

"Would you like some tea or–" Felicia began.

Their guest shook her head.

"I came to talk."

"I see."

"When I was here two – three days ago, I was so angry I did not speak English," she continued with great difficulty.

The girls waited, their pulses quickening.

"I am very angry that my children come here," the woman said. "I do not like it when they hear religion."

"But–" Joan started to protest.

However, their Dutch guest did not give her time to finish.

"Yesterday, I saw men come here. At first I thought I would not tell on them, but maybe it is bad for you if I do not tell. Maybe it is very bad."

"You mean you saw the men who told the boys they were from the telephone company and got into the boat?"

She nodded.

"Since Tuenis and Wil said they want to come here, I keep a watch to see if they do. Yesterday this Volkswagen comes up and stops, and two men get out. They talk to the boys. Have them unlock boat and go inside. In a few minutes, they rush back out, get into car, and drive away. Very fast!"

"We appreciate your telling us all this," Felicia said, "but we had already contacted the phone company and found out that they didn't work for them. Fortunately, however, they didn't steal anything."

The woman's face was white and drawn.

"That you know," she said in broken English. "This you do not know."

She spread a Dutch newspaper before them and pointed to a picture of two men on the front page.

"These men!" she exclaimed, her voice rising.

"They go on your boat! *These* men!" She jabbed at the paper for emphasis.

Felicia and Joan stared at the pictures.

"But who are they?" Felicia asked. "And what have they done to get their names in the paper?"

Abruptly the woman got to her feet.

"Very bad men!" she exclaimed. And with that she turned and stalked away.

Time seemed to stop while Felicia and Joan stared after their departed guest. Felicia was breathing heavily, and her shoulders were trembling.

"What do you suppose that means?" she asked, forcing out the words between gritted teeth.

"It sure doesn't sound good," Joan replied. "If Amsterdam's like Boston, they don't put a person's picture on the front page for helping old ladies across the street or teaching Sunday school."

Mechanically, Felicia got to her feet.

"We've got to get hold of a copy of that newspaper," she said. "That's the first thing."

"We'd better hurry before they're gone."

They locked the boat once more and went down the canal toward the sea until they came to a newsstand. For a moment or two when they couldn't find the paper, dismay all but overwhelmed them.

"There's none here!" Joan exclaimed.

"And we didn't even think to get the name of it," Felicia said, "so we don't know what to ask for."

She moved around to the other side of the little newsstand.

"May I help you?" a pleasant voice asked in perfect English.

Both girls' heads snapped up. They stared at the smiling stranger.

"You–you're an American," Joan blurted.

"In a way," he said, laughing. "What paper are you looking for?"

"We don't know the name of it," Felicia said, "but it is today's paper, and it has the pictures of two men on the front page."

The stranger spoke to the newsman in Dutch. He nodded and shrugged his shoulders.

"He says he's sorry, but he's all sold out. Everybody, it seems, is interested in the smuggling ring that's been uncovered."

"Smuggling ring?" In spite of herself, Felicia gasped.

"You are surprised?" he asked. "Those things happen in other countries besides America, you know."

While she was fumbling uncertainly for words, he picked a paper from the stand and dropped a note in the vendor's hand.

"Here," he said. His smile had disappeared, and his eyes smoldered darkly. "You can read about it in English – with my compliments."

He left them abruptly and got on a streetcar that had just stopped nearby.

"I thought he was nice," Felicia said after a moment

or two. "But when he handed me this paper – brrrr. He stared right through me!"

"Did you see the paper in his pocket?" Joan asked, her voice expressionless. "It was the same one Tuenis's mother had with her when she called on us this afternoon."

"That probably doesn't mean anything except that he can read Dutch as well as speak it."

"But he looked familiar," Joan protested. "He looked exactly like the picture of one of the men on the front page of that paper!"

The color drained from Felicia's cheeks. Fear snatched her breath and left her weak and trembling.

"Are you sure?" she demanded.

"Didn't you *see* it?"

Felicia managed a little, mouth-twisting grin. "Now, who's trying to frighten whom?"

"I've been associating with you so much I'm becoming a detective too," Joan said. "You've got me suspecting everyone I see."

"Joan Bailey!" her friend scolded. "Be serious!"

"I am serious." She lowered her voice. "I honestly think that stranger who bought the paper for us just now has his picture on the front page of today's paper!"

"But I don't see how he'd dare to be out in public if that's true," Felicia countered. "If you recognized him that easily, you'd think the police would spot him too and arrest him."

"Maybe they haven't seen the papers yet."

In spite of herself, Felicia laughed.

"What do you think we ought to do?" Joan persisted. "Go to the police?"

Felicia tugged thoughtfully at the lobe of her ear. "I think we'd better find another newsstand first and see if we can get a copy of that paper. We'd feel awfully foolish going to the police again with another false alarm."

They left the street that paralleled the canal and crossed over three blocks to locate another newsstand.

"Here it is!" Joan cried, jerking a paper from the rack.

Felicia paid for it while Joan stared at the pictures in the middle of the page.

"This is the one," she whispered.

Felicia took her arm.

"Let's go back to the boat before we look at it," she said. "Everybody's watching us."

The girls made their way hurriedly through the early evening crowds. Once they were on the boat, Joan shut the door hurriedly, locked it, and turned to the kitchen table.

"Now just take a look," she said, her voice tensing as she spread the paper out on the table between them. "Isn't this the guy who came up and talked to us?"

For a moment or two, Felicia examined the picture carefully.

"It does look a bit like him," she said at last, "but the one in this picture has gray hair and a mustache."

"Some hair dye and a razor would take care of them."

Felicia switched on the light and once more turned back to the picture.

"This one looks quite a bit heavier," she observed, "and not nearly as dignified as the man who bought the paper for us. I don't think they're the same person at all."

Disappointment flickered in Joan's eyes.

"Well, I do." She sat down at the table and picked up the newspaper. "I wish I could read this story," she said thoughtfully.

Felicia did not reply. She was looking at the English paper the stranger had bought them.

"Listen to this, Joan." She began reading, "'Customs officials in Amsterdam disclosed today that a gigantic diamond smuggling ring has been uncovered. The announcement was made after the arrest of an American woman tourist with $200,000 worth of undeclared diamonds in her possession. Police have refused to disclose her name, address, or any other information pending further investigation.'"

Joan gasped.

"Two hundred thousand dollars' worth of diamonds!" she exclaimed. "So that's what they were looking for when they searched our baggage. I'm sure glad they didn't find any."

"Listen to this, 'However, it was revealed by usually informed sources that she is believed to be part of a larger ring of international smugglers. Jon Buerger of Rotterdam and Nicholas Sweeney, an American whose last known address was Leopoldville, the Republic of Congo, are being sought for questioning. It is believed they are in Amsterdam or the vicinity.'"

Slowly she folded the paper and laid it aside.

"Those are the names of the two men in this picture," Felicia observed, her voice faltering. "The two men Tuenis and Wil's mother said she saw come to the Bible Boat yesterday."

"She could have been mistaken about those men," Joan said uncertainly. "I'm sure she only got a glimpse of them."

"That's not what she said. She was watching the boat to be sure her kids didn't come aboard. Remember? She'd have seen them from the time they got out of their car until they left the boat and drove away."

Felicia crossed to the door and looked out on the busy street for a moment or two.

"It gives me the cold chills just to think about it," her friend said.

"You're not alone," Felicia told her. "But why would two men like that come here to the boat? That's what I can't figure out. We don't know anything about any smuggling, and I'm sure the missionaries don't either."

Joan nodded.

"That's why I wondered if Wil's mother could have been mistaken. This doesn't make sense."

Somebody stepped from the canal bank to the boat. Both girls started.

"Wh-wh-who's there?" Felicia managed.

"It's just us!"

The girls sighed their relief, and Joan went over and opened the door.

Karlje's young face was white with fear.

"You've got to come over to our clubhouse right away," he whispered.

"But why?" Joan asked curiously.

"Uncle Hans is there! He says he's got to see you right away!"

Felicia and Joan both stared at the frightened boy.

"He told us that we should come quick and get you," the Dutch boy continued. "He said it's a matter of life and death!"

There was a brief, taut silence.

"Now just what happened?" Felicia asked. "Sit down and start at the beginning. Tell us everything that took place."

"We haven't got time for that," Karlje blurted. "He said for us to hurry!"

"Well," Felicia retorted, "I can tell him this much – we're not going out to meet him until we know exactly what the situation is and what he wants."

"That's for sure!" Joan added.

"We had Wil and Tuenis inside having Bible club for them," Karlje began, "when Uncle Hans came."

"He was so scared he crowded inside right during club," Steve added. "We could hardly breathe."

"We *couldn't* stop club right then," Karlje said. "We were in the middle of the Bible lesson. So Steve went outside, and I finished. As soon as the kids were gone, Uncle Hans said I should come and get you. He said if I didn't get you over there right away, something terrible would happen to him."

The girls looked at each other quizzically.

"What do you think, Felicia?" the other girl asked. "Should we go or not?"

"You've got to!" Karlje broke in desperately.

CHAPTER 9

UNCLE HANS' SECRET

There was a long, breathless silence. The only sound in the Bible Boat was that of the water slapping gently on the hull.

"If we go over there," Felicia said after what must have seemed a very long time, "will you boys go with us?"

There was another short hesitation. Steve's gaze met Karlje's.

"How about it?"

"I–I will if Karlje does," he said finally.

Karlje nodded.

"And I'll go if you will, Steve."

"I should think you would," Joan put in. "After all, it's your uncle you want us to go over to see."

Felicia got her sweater, switched off the lights, and followed the trio off the boat.

"I'm glad it's not too late," Joan shuddered glancing

around with growing uneasiness. "There are still a lot of people on the street. That's one good thing."

"Not where we're going" Karlje observed. "Nobody much walks around over there. It's too dark."

Joan shivered.

"That's why Uncle Hans wanted you to come over there. Nobody'd see him."

"And what about us?" she asked. "Nobody'd see if we got hit on the head or kidnapped either."

"Joan," Felicia scolded. "Don't talk that way. You'll frighten Steve and Karlje."

"If I do, there'll be three of us scared." She eyed her friend obliquely.

They walked on for several minutes. Steadily, Felicia increased her pace until they were practically running up the sidewalk.

"What's the hurry?" Joan asked, panting. "You're going to kill us all off if you're not careful."

"We can't waste any time. Remember what Karlje's Uncle Hans said about our hurrying. Every minute counts."

"I am thinking about what he said," Joan retorted. "And every time I think about it, I want to go even slower."

The streets they had been walking along were well lighted until they turned onto the narrow, twisting street where the boys had built their clubhouse. The darkness was a curtain stretching from one house and storefront to another, blotting out entryways and hiding windows, except those that were lighted. And even then, the lights were dim, as though waging an uneven, losing battle against the night.

Felicia looked apprehensively over her shoulder and hurried on. This time there was no protest from Joan. She was at least a pace and a half ahead.

When they reached the makeshift clubhouse, Joan stopped.

"Uncle Hans," Karlje whispered. "Uncle Hans, we're here!"

No answer.

"Uncle Hans!" The boy's voice increased in volume. "We're back with Felicia and Joan!"

Still all was silence from within.

"Maybe he's asleep," Joan blurted.

"I'll get him." Steve stooped and crawled inside. A moment later, he poked his head out. "He's not in here, Karlje!"

"But he's got to be! He said he'd wait here until we brought the girls."

Steve came out and stood upright. "You can look for yourself if you want to. He's not in there."

"Maybe you didn't understand him correctly, Karlje," Felicia said. "Are you sure he wanted to meet us here?"

"That's what he said," Steve put in. "He told us two or three times that we should go and get you and bring you here."

"Well," Joan answered, "he must not have wanted

to see us very badly or he'd have waited until we got over here. We came as quickly as we could."

"Something must've happened to him," Karlje said with concern in his voice, "or he'd have been here."

Felicia took a long, deep breath. Her mouth opened as though to speak, but she stopped suddenly.

"Listen!" she whispered tautly.

Somebody was walking toward them in the darkness. The sound of footsteps was very audible.

"Somebody's coming!" Joan said. "Maybe it's Karlje's Uncle Hans."

"And maybe the person out there is the reason Uncle Hans isn't here!" Felicia grabbed Karlje's arm and jerked him around. "Let's get back to the boat as fast as we can!"

Shoving the boy ahead of her, she broke into a run. Joan and Steve did the same. The stranger in the darkness started to run too. He gained on them but stopped when they reached the safety of the well-lit street.

Felicia slowed to a walk. Joan turned and stared at her.

"Are you out of your mind?" she asked incredulously. "That guy's not half a block behind us."

"We're not going to have to worry about him on a busy street like this."

"I–I hope you're right."

"So-so do I," Steve put in.

Although they kept glancing back from time to time, there was no sign of whoever had been following them.

"It almost seems like a dream," Felicia said, unlocking the door to the Bible Boat and fumbling for the light.

"Not to me, it doesn't," Joan retorted firmly.

Slowly Karlje took off his jacket and hung it up.

"I sure wish I knew what happened to my Uncle Hans," he said thoughtfully.

"So do I," Joan answered, "but not enough to want to go out and find him."

They were just finishing dinner that evening when there was a light tap on the kitchen window. Joan jerked upright.

"Wh-what was that?" she demanded.

For the space of a minute, a breathless silence hung over the little table. Then the tapping came again. It was subdued but sharp – urgent.

"I think there's somebody out there." Felicia pushed the chair back and got to her feet.

"What're you going to do?" her friend demanded.

"I'm going to see who it is of course."

"Felicia!" Horror edged Joan's voice. "Don't you *dare* open that door!"

But Felicia did not slacken her pace. At the door, however, she spoke guardedly.

"Who is it? What do you want?"

"It's me! Hans!" Desperation laced the words. "Let me in. I have got to talk to you!"

"You were supposed to meet us at Karlje and Steve's clubhouse."

"I couldn't stay there." His voice broke. "They were closing in on me! They'd have gotten me if I'd stayed."

"Who's after you?" Felicia persisted. "The police?"

"No!" The word exploded from his lips. "Not the police! I am not in trouble with the police." He tried the locked door. "Please, lady. Let me in! If they catch me out here, they'll–"

Suddenly making up her mind, she unlocked the door and removed the guard chain. A slight, ashen faced young man slipped in.

"Thank you," he breathed. "Thank you!" For an instant, he leaned against the door, gasping painfully to ease the burning of his lungs. "Lock the door," he ordered, "and draw the blinds. If–if they see me in here, it might be too bad for all of us!"

The boys sprang to the windows while Felicia put the guard chain in place to secure the door.

After a couple of minutes, their frightened visitor seemed to have caught his breath. His chest was no longer heaving rhythmically, and the color was coming back to his face. He could speak without effort.

"I–I'm sorry to barge in on you like this," he said, finally. "But I didn't know where to turn. I'm in trouble. Bad trouble!"

Felicia's expression did not soften.

"Perhaps you had better start at the beginning and tell us exactly what this is all about," she said coolly.

"I–I am not sure I can tell you everything," he hedged.

"Then tell us as much as you can."

He tried to swallow the lump in his throat.

"Of course," he said numbly. "Of course, you want to know what is going on. You've got a right to know. But what I'm going to tell you will probably sound unbelievable to you even though it is the truth."

The little audience waited tensely.

"Karlje probably told you that I am an artist," he began, "or that I am trying to be."

The girls nodded.

"He also said you've been in and out of jail quite a lot," Joan said bluntly.

The corners of his mouth twitched, and, for an instant, he seemed to forget what he was saying.

"I have been in jail," he acknowledged lamely. "I do not know what that has got to do with what I am telling you, but I do not deny it. I have been in jail for being drunk and fighting or disturbing the peace. But that is all. I swear it. I have never done anything really bad."

"I'd call that bad enough," Joan retorted.

"The Bible says that all have sinned and come short of the glory of God," Felicia reminded him gently.

If she had slapped him, he could not have been more surprised. He flinched at her words, and it was half a minute or so before he could speak again.

"That is what Karlje said to those kids in the Bible club," he muttered, as though to himself.

"That isn't all we were telling the kids in club," Karlje went on. "The Bible says, *The wages of sin is death.* But Tante Joka always reminds us that it doesn't stop there. It says, *But the gift of God is eternal life through Jesus Christ our Lord.* "

Briefly, conviction blazed in the frightened young man's eyes, and he fought against it.

"But that–that is not what I came here to–to talk about right now," he blurted. "I–I have not had much money to spend for supplies, so I–I have been buying them from this shopkeeper across from the newsstand on the canal. His reputation is not too good. But he does have good paints, and he sells his frames and canvases cheap."

"And that's where you got the canvas and frame for the painting I bought. Is that right?" Joan asked him.

He nodded.

"And that is when my trouble started. I do not know whether he gave me something he shouldn't or what happened, but about the time I finished the painting, somebody tried to break into my room. Somebody followed me. So, I thought I would put a stop to it. I sold the painting to you."

"So that's why you sold it so cheaply," Joan concluded.

"And why we were followed and the Bible Boat broken into," Felicia added.

"I did not tell them you bought the painting from me. They found out some other way."

"We didn't make any effort to keep it a secret," Joan acknowledged. "Quite a few people saw it. We even took it to an art critic to have it appraised."

"Somehow they found out you had my painting," he went on breathlessly. "But it was not until they got on the Bible Boat and didn't find it here that they–they came to my apartment." He swallowed painfully. "And they–they told me that I have to get the painting back for them or they will hit me on the head and throw me in the canal."

"We wouldn't want that to happen," Joan said.

"Neither would I. It sounds very uncomfortable."

"What is it you want us to do?" Felicia asked him.

"A simple thing. If you will give me back the painting, I will return your thirty euros and we will all forget this ever happened."

"Do you suppose this is involved in the diamond smuggling in some way?" Felicia asked abruptly.

"What it is involved in, I do not know," he said, eyeing the door carefully. "Nor do I want to. All I want is to stop them from breaking into my apartment and following me around and breaking my head open maybe."

"Why don't you go to the police and tell them your story?" she asked. "Information like this might help them to catch the smugglers. And it would solve your problem as far as they're concerned at the same time."

He gasped at the thought.

"Me, go to the police?" he echoed. "And just how long do you think it would take a person with a reputation like mine to make them believe me? If I showed up at their door, they would lock me up and that would be the end of that."

He inhaled deeply.

"So, if you will give me back the painting, I will give you your thirty euros and we will all forget any of this ugly business ever happened."

Joan's gaze met Felicia's.

"I couldn't give you your painting even if I wanted to," she said. "I mailed it to America this afternoon."

He stared at her incredulously.

"No," he said, scarcely mouthing the words. "You do not mean it. You–you are just joking."

"I'm not saying I'd give it to you to turn over to those smugglers anyway," she countered, "but that really doesn't make any difference one way or the other. It's gone now!"

He stared blankly at her.

"You–you mean you mailed it to America?" he repeated as though there must have been some mistake.

"That's right. It's probably on a jet bound for Boston right now."

Time seemed to stop for Karlje's Uncle Hans. The lights in his eyes flickered out, and the color seeped from his cheeks leaving them sallow and lifeless. Perspiration beaded his hairline, and his thin hands began to tremble nervously.

"On the way to Boston," he repeated. "They will never believe me! No matter how hard I try, they will *never* believe I am telling the truth!"

He got up and started for the door.

"They will *never* believe me!"

CHAPTER 10

FELICIA'S PLAN

Felicia, Joan, and the two boys silently watched Karlje's Uncle Hans leave the Bible Boat. He hesitated at the door once more, looking back appealingly. Then he was gone. It was a minute or two before anyone spoke.

"A person can't help feeling sorry for him," Felicia said pensively.

"But I'm glad the painting had been mailed to America," Joan said. "As a Christian, I couldn't have given it to him."

The corners of Felicia's mouth tightened.

"Well," Joan said suddenly, "what is it, Felicia? What's the big pronouncement?"

"What do you mean?" Felicia asked.

"I've seen those symptoms before. What is it you're thinking about?"

She laughed self-consciously. "As a matter of fact,"

she continued, "I *was* thinking about something. I was wondering if it actually is the painting that those smugglers are after."

"You heard Uncle Hans," Joan said. "How could it be anything else?"

"I was just thinking about what he said. If he was telling the truth, he didn't know – and still doesn't know – why anyone should want the painting. So, what he concerned himself with was the canvas and the paint."

"I still don't see what you're driving at."

"We took the stretched canvas painting out of the frame," Felicia said. "That's what we mailed to Boston. And there was nothing in or on the canvas we mailed to your dad that any smugglers or anyone else would want – except for the picture. And that couldn't have any diamonds in it!"

Briefly, Joan stared at her.

"But there's *got* to be something about the painting or the frame or something to make those men so desperate to get it back."

Felicia jerked upright.

"Joan!" she cried. "That's it!"

Blankly, her friend eyed her.

"What's what?" she asked curiously.

"Do you remember that peculiar piece of cardboard that served as a backing to the frame?" she continued. "The one with the floor plan of an apartment on it and several rows of street numbers printed underneath?"

"I remember that you mentioned something about it," Joan said, "but I didn't pay any attention to it." Momentarily, her eyes gleamed. "But how could that have anything to do with the smugglers?"

"That's what I don't know," Felicia retorted. "But we're going to find out!"

She disappeared into their bedroom.

"Joan," she called, moments later, "what did you do with that frame?"

"I put it in the closet. Why?"

Felicia was standing in the doorway.

"It's not here," she said numbly. "It's gone!" Her attractive young face paled. "They got it after all!"

"But they couldn't have!" Joan went to the bedroom herself. "It was just a few hours ago that I took the painting out of it and set it in there. Somebody's been here practically ever since. They *couldn't* have gotten in here and stolen it!"

"It's gone just the same. Look for yourself."

Steve Calverley and Karlje were eyeing one another uneasily.

"What're you talking about?" Steve asked at last. "The frame Uncle Hans's oil painting was in?"

"That's right. Do you know where it is?"

"Well–" he gulped hard. "Sort of."

"You see, we didn't have anything in our clubhouse like a picture or a plaque," Karlje broke in.

"And we thought you wouldn't mind if we borrowed the frame and–and wrote our own plaque in crayon on the piece of cardboard."

"And it's in your clubhouse?" Felicia echoed.

"We didn't mean any harm," Steve said quickly. "Honest we didn't. We just wanted a plaque that said, 'Jesus saves' in Dutch so the kids could see it when they first got inside. Only we didn't have any money to buy one, so-so–" His voice trailed away.

Felicia smiled reassuringly.

"That's perfectly all right. We're just glad that it's where it is instead of in the hands of those smugglers."

"At least we know where it is," Joan said. "The first thing in the morning, we can go down and get it. We can soon see if we can figure out why those smugglers would be so anxious to get their big mitts on it. If that is what they're after."

"It's what they're after, all right," Felicia said firmly. "It's got to be."

Fear flickered in Karlje's eyes.

"But what about my Uncle Hans?" he demanded. "What'll they do to him between now and morning?"

The corners of Joan's lips tightened.

"I'd never thought of that."

It was a full minute before anyone spoke again.

"It wouldn't take me very long to go and get that picture frame," Karlje suggested. "I hung it myself, so I know right where it is."

There was no color in Steve's face, but he spoke bravely.

"I'll go with you."

"Oh, no, you won't!" Joan exclaimed. "You boys aren't going out on that dark street alone!"

"But Uncle Hans!"

"Even if we did have the frame and knew why they're so anxious to get it, we couldn't turn it over to your Uncle Hans. It wouldn't be honest. It would be breaking the law. We'd have to go to the police with it."

"But if the police had it, they might be able to catch those men before they got to do something terrible to Uncle Hans. Or maybe they would p-pro-tect him."

"But we just can't let you go over to that clubhouse alone tonight," Joan countered. "We wouldn't think of it, would we, Felicia?"

"That's right," Felicia answered. "It would be out of the question to let the boys go alone." She inhaled deeply. "But we could go with them."

Astonishment widened Joan's eyes.

"What?"

"Karlje's right about his Uncle Hans, Joan," she continued. "Those smugglers are desperate criminals. There's no telling what they might do to him."

"There's no telling what they might do to the four of us, either – if they ever get their hands on us." She shuddered.

"It won't take more than fifteen minutes," Felicia assured her.

"And a lot of things can happen in fifteen minutes," Joan said. "How long do you think it would take them to bop us on the head and toss us in the canal or stick a knife in our ribs?"

Felicia laughed.

"You sound to me as though you've been reading too many of the wrong kind of comic books."

Joan made a little face at her.

"Have you forgotten?" she asked. "We proper Wellington girls do not read comic books. We spend our time in more wholesome pursuits. Like going up dark streets at night and running the risk of getting our scalps lifted."

"Oh, quit complaining and get your jacket," Felicia said good-naturedly. "The boys and I are all ready to go."

"All right," Joan said, sighing her resignation. "I'll go along this time. But you're going to keep getting me into things like this until you wind up getting me killed. Then we'll both be sorry."

Felicia took the key from her purse.

"I think we'd better leave the lights on," she said, "so if anybody comes by, they'll think we're here."

They stepped out in the cool night air, and Felicia closed and locked the door behind them. The four of them walked quickly up the street. The crowds that had been present earlier had thinned greatly. Here and there someone hurried by to catch a streetcar or a girl and boy walked slowly along the canal, scarcely aware of the fact that anyone else in the world existed.

On any other occasion Joan would have nudged Felicia and made a remark. But not this evening. Their errand was too serious – too filled with danger.

"See anyone following us?" she whispered.

Felicia shook her head.

"All's quiet behind us, in front of us, and on either side."

"You hope."

"Why be such a pessimist?"

"I'm just being a realist," Joan continued. "That's all."

They quickened their pace slightly as they entered the dark street, but there was still no sign of anyone following them. It wasn't long until they reached the little, makeshift clubhouse.

"Well," Joan said with a nervous giggle, "here we are.

"I'll get it," Karlje said, stooping to enter the shack he and Steve had built.

He began to grope around in the darkness.

"Have you found it yet?" Steve whispered tensely.

"It's dark in here."

"Let me help you," Felicia said. Taking a small pen flashlight from her purse, she went into the clubhouse.

When she flicked on the light, the faint beam illuminated a small circle on the opposite wall and chased the darkness from a portion of the clubhouse interior. The boys had done quite an acceptable job with the materials they had – old packing cases, sticks of used lumber, and a couple of squares of water-soaked fiberboard they'd picked up somewhere. And on the wall nearest the building, hung the picture frame with its neatly crayoned motto in Dutch.

"There it is, Karlje!" Felicia whispered tautly. "Hand it to me."

There was a long moment of waiting. Joan, who was standing outside with Steve, looked about with growing uneasiness.

"Felicia!" she whispered. "Come on! We've got to get out of here!"

"In just a minute."

"You can look at it when we get back to the Bible B–"

Joan didn't get to finish what she was saying. A tall figure emerged out of the darkness and pressed close to her.

"Well," a familiar voice said icily. "If it isn't the friend I met at the newsstand."

Involuntarily, Joan screamed. The man's hand snaked out and grasped her by the wrist.

"I wouldn't try that again if I were you!" he rasped. "We don't want to hurt you, but we're not above doing it if you give us any trouble."

Steve, who had been standing there transfixed by fear, whirled and started to dash away. But a pair of strong arms enveloped him, and a harsh voice hissed in Dutch.

The man holding Joan spoke hurriedly in Dutch to the one who seemed to materialize out of nowhere to grab Steve. All she could understand was the name. Jon! That was the name of the Dutch half of the brains behind the gang of smugglers! She had been right after all. The man who had captured her must be Nick Sweeney!

"Now, do as you're told, and you won't get hurt," he whispered in her ear. "Tell your friend and the Dutch kid who's in there with her to come out quietly."

Felicia and Karlje, who had been listening to the interchange, did as he demanded.

"Now, that's better." An evil grin twisted the man's face. "If you do as you're told, it'll be better for all of us."

CHAPTER II

DRIVE TO THE COUNTRY

"**W**h-what're you going to do to us?" Steve blurted.
"That all depends on how well you cooperate with us," Nick Sweeney said. "If you do as we ask, you will be treated very well indeed. If you don't–" He shrugged his shoulders expressively. "Who knows what we will have to do to get your help?"

By this time, a large car had pulled into the street at the end of the block and was approaching them with its lights off.

"You're not going to be able to get away with this, you know," Felicia told him.

"Let us worry about that."

"You're in bad enough trouble already without adding kidnapping to it."

The tall American laughed mirthlessly.

"You are only half right, young lady. We have many charges against us, it is true. But not so many we don't *dare* to add kidnapping to them. It is more nearly correct to say we have so many charges against us that it doesn't make much difference what else we do, including kidnapping."

"The Dutch have a very good police force," Joan said, defiance flaming in her dark eyes. "If you kidnap us, they'll have you arrested before morning."

"They have been trying to arrest us for weeks," he murmured. "But you need have no fear, young lady, we're not going to kidnap you. We just want to talk to you in a nice, quiet place about something you've got that we've got to have. That's all. I wouldn't call it kidnapping."

"The police will."

"The police will know nothing about it. And you will all be released without harm if you give us your complete cooperation."

The car glided to a halt beside them, and the one called Jon opened the door.

"Now, please get in," Nick said as quietly and as genially as he had spoken to them earlier in the evening. "We'd like to take you for that short ride we've been talking about."

"And if we don't?" Joan demanded. Her feet were planted wide apart stubbornly, and her eyes blazed.

His gaze met hers. In silence, they fought.

"You'll wish you had," he snarled.

Joan was in no mood to surrender so easily, but Felicia nudged her.

"Come on, Joan," she said quietly. "We're in no position to argue."

"Now there's a smart young lady," Nick said. "You listen to her, sis, and you won't get into trouble."

Joan got into the car. As she did so, she gasped audibly. But Karlje was the one who spoke aloud.

"Uncle Hans!" he cried.

"Shut up!"

The driver whirled and would have clouted him on the side of the head, but Joan jerked him back just in time.

"Don't you dare lay a hand on him!" she exploded. "Don't you *dare* touch either of these boys!"

"A little spitfire, eh?" The driver laughed.

But Nick Sweeney spoke sharply to him in Dutch.

"I–I'm sorry," the driver stammered abjectly. "It won't happen again."

"It had better not!"

The American smuggler got in behind Felicia and Steve and closed the door. Immediately, the car began to move away.

"Leo is the hotheaded one of our group," Nick said. "But as long as everything goes our way – as long as you do as we ask – you will have nothing to fear from him. I can assure you that he will try nothing more like that."

But they were scarcely listening to the smuggler. All four of them were staring at the tightly bound man on the floor of the bus.

"You recognize Karlje's Uncle Hans, no?" the American said. "Unfortunately, he would not cooperate with us, so we had to tie him."

Hans was staring up at Nick with hostile eyes.

"I am so very sorry," Sweeney went on after a moment or two, "but I must draw the blinds. It would not be good for you to see where we are going."

They rode for half an hour or more without stopping. They must have gone into the country because the driver increased his speed and held it there. At last, the car pulled to a stop, and the driver turned in the seat.

"We will blindfold them, eh, Nick?"

"I think that would be most expedient. It is better to give them no information at all that could be used against us than to have to see that they do not inform the authorities about us."

The driver and Nick blindfolded the four of them and Hans. Only then did they let them get out of the car.

"It would be better to take hold of hands," Nick said. "The ground is rough. We wouldn't want you to fall."

The one called Leo laughed as though the smuggler had just told a good joke.

"No," he said. "We wouldn't want you to fall until after we've got what we need from you."

The tone in his voice chilled Felicia thoroughly.

The little group of captives was led over a short

stretch of plowed ground, across a wooden bridge of some sort, and into a wooden structure. This last Felicia learned by feeling the wall as they went through the door.

"Now, we will go upstairs," Nick said. "I think it will be quieter for us there."

He led them up three short flights of stairs.

"We will leave Hans here," the smuggler continued. "The rest of you will go on with us."

He took them up two more flights of stairs, securely locked the door, and had Leo remove the blindfolds. For a moment or two, Felicia, Joan, and the boys blinked, their eyes struggling to adjust to the dim light.

Felicia looked slowly around. They were in a small room with steeply slanted sides.

"Now," Nick began, his entire manner changing. "Where is the oil painting you bought from Hans?"

"On its way to America to my father," Joan retorted in defiance. "What do you think you can do about that?"

"You lie!"

"I'm telling you the truth," she answered quickly.

"I tell you that Caisse is the one who lied to us!" Leo broke in. "He wants those diamonds for himself!"

"Shut up! Caisse didn't even know about the frame von Steuben left with him. That's how he came to make a mistake and sell it to Hans."

At the mention of the frame, Karlje gasped.

Nick saw it!

"Ah-ha!" He almost leaped to where the boy was standing. "You know about the frame, yes?"

Karlje's face flushed lividly, but he said nothing.

"You know about the frame!" Nicholas grasped the boy's arm and wrenched it savagely.

Joan sprang forward, but Leo grasped her and pinned her arms to her sides.

"Now, tell us about the frame," Nick went on, "or you'll really get hurt! And that's a promise!"

"Don't!" Felicia cried. "Don't hurt him. I–I have the frame here in my purse."

"So!" Triumph gleamed evilly in Nick's eyes. "I thought you didn't lie to me!"

"I didn't," Joan retorted. "You asked about the painting. I don't have it. I mailed it to my dad in America."

Numbly, Felicia opened her purse and gave him the frame. Leo and Jon both crowded close to stare at it.

CHAPTER 12

FROM THE WINDMILL

Leo and Jon crowded close to Nick Sweeney staring down at the picture frame in his trembling hands.

"Is that the one?" Leo demanded.

"There's Caisse's name on the back. It's the frame all right."

"But–but there's no wire," Leo protested weakly. "No map. Nothing."

Jon spoke rapidly in Dutch, and for a minute or so, the conversation was in that language. Then Nick turned his attention to the picture frame once more.

"That Caisse!" he exploded. "He did not put the wire or the map on the frame! Somehow, he found out about them and what they meant and decided to keep them for himself!"

Anger twisted Leo's face.

"That's what I've been trying to tell you!" he

retorted savagely. "I told you from the start that we couldn't trust him."

"Shut up!" Nick whirled to face Felicia. "Do you have that wire?" he demanded.

"What would I do with picture frame wire?" she asked innocently.

Without answering, he jerked the purse from her and dumped it on the floor. Pens, aspirin, small change, her New Testament, and assorted small items she had been hoarding scattered at her feet.

"You didn't have to do that," she sputtered indignantly. "I told you I didn't have it!"

Nick Sweeney snatched up the frame, grasped it on either side with his big hands, and wrenched it apart. In one savage motion, he hurled it against the wall.

"That is what I'll do to Caisse when I get my hands on him!"

Jon spoke again earnestly, and Nick turned to the driver.

"That's right, Leo. You'd better stay here and keep an eye on our–our guests until we're sure we're through with them."

His eyes narrowed suspiciously.

"You wouldn't be running out on me, now would you?"

"I'm not even going to answer that!" Nick said. "You just keep your eyes open so you're sure they're all here when Jon and I get back."

Leo waited only until he heard Nicholas and Jon drive away.

"I'm going to be right downstairs," he warned darkly. "And I sleep light, so I don't think it would be wise for you to try any funny stuff. See?"

The girls, Steve, and Karlje eyed him but said nothing as he left. He slammed the door behind him, and a moment later, the lock clicked into place. They heard gradually fading footsteps on the stairs.

"He's gone!" Steve exclaimed in a hoarse whisper. "He's gone!"

"That's a relief," Felicia said.

"I still don't have the foggiest notion of what this is all about," Joan put in. "If these two characters are smugglers, why wouldn't they have the diamonds themselves? Why would they be trying so hard to find out where the stones are?"

"They were talking about that in Dutch," Karlje explained. "I guess they forgot about my being here or that I'm Dutch and would know what they were saying. The way I understand it, they had other people to do the smuggling. They just got the stuff and figured how to get it into the country."

"They sound like that sort," Joan said. "They want somebody else to get arrested if the deal goes sour."

"I guess they don't know exactly how the authorities found out about the diamond smuggling," Karlje went on, "or how they happened to arrest that woman. But they had a plan worked out in case there was trouble before this von Steuben person, whoever he is, had to sneak out of Holland before he got a chance to turn the diamonds over to them. He was to put them in a safe hiding place and leave a map marking the location on a picture frame in the art shop this Caisse guy operates."

"So that explains it," Felicia said.

"Caisse was just supposed to have kept the frame there and give it to them when they came in, but he or one of his clerks sold it to Uncle Hans. And he used it to frame the oil painting he'd just finished."

"I see," Felicia observed thoughtfully. "That explains a lot of things. We know why they were after your Uncle Hans and why they started following us and breaking into the boat when he told them he'd sold the painting to Joan."

Joan turned to her friend.

"I almost died when they started talking about that map and the wire, Felicia," she said. "There was a wire on that frame when I bought it, and you saw the map, so it was there too. What did you do with them anyway?"

Karlje grinned broadly.

"I've got the wire wrapped around my ankle and tied under my sock," he said. "They never would have found it. That's what Felicia and I were doing in the clubhouse that took so long."

"What made you even think about the wire?" Joan asked.

"I remembered that the wires had been taken off the pictures in the boat when we were broken into by those fake telephone men. I figured maybe they were after those wires for some reason."

"That explains the wire," Joan answered. "But what about the map? Where's it? Did you chew it up and swallow it?"

"Nothing like that." Felicia slipped off her shoe. "I just folded it up and put it in here for safekeeping."

She took the piece of cardboard from her shoe, unfolded it, and spread it out on the floor. Joan and the two boys knelt beside her, peering intently down at it.

"Just what has this got to do with locating those diamonds?" Joan asked. "That's what I can't figure out."

Felicia ran the short piece of knotted wire thoughtfully through her fingers.

"There are two knots in this soft wire," she muttered, more to herself than to her companions. "And there are two parts to this map. That could be significant, but I don't know how."

"Say," Steve observed, "there's something here I didn't see before. Look at this little red dot down at the bottom of the cardboard. Do you suppose that means anything?"

"It could be," Felicia said. "It just could be."

She held the wire up to examine it in the narrow shaft of light that was coming from the window high above them.

"There's a nick in the loop at this end of the wire,"

she said. "And it's got some red paint or coloring in it. That must mean those two go together in some way. Let's try something."

Putting a pencil in the loop in that end of the wire, she placed the pencil point on the red dot. Then she stretched the wire until the other end reached the opposite corner of the sheet of cardboard.

"Look!" she cried softly.

One knot fell exactly on a certain street number in the list below the apartment plan. The other marked a spot in the corner of the living room nearest the kitchen.

"I see it all now, Felicia!" Joan exclaimed, excitement tinging her voice. "This knot marks the location of the apartment where the diamonds are hidden. They're at this address. And this one marks the location of the diamond cache in the apartment."

There was a brief silence.

"We've got to get this information to the police quick."

"But how? We're still locked up. Or have you forgotten?"

"There's got to be some way out of here," Felicia said, walking about the small, oddly shaped room. She turned to Karlje. "You look as though you're lighter than Steve. Do you think you could climb up on my shoulders and look out?"

"I think so."

He took off his shoes, and Joan helped him get his feet on Felicia's shoulders.

"See anything?" she asked.

"Not yet." He grasped the windowsill and hoisted himself higher. "Yes. We're out in the country in the top of an old windmill. I can see the wheel."

"An old windmill?" Joan echoed.

"That's right."

"But it's so big."

"People live in some of them," he observed, getting down.

"This isn't going to do us much good to know that we're in a windmill," Joan said. "We're still locked up tight."

"Just a minute," Felicia broke in. "I think I'm getting an idea."

Joan eyed her quizzically.

"I don't like it when you get that look on your face."

"This won't be too hard for you."

"What won't be too hard for me?"

"The wheels on these windmills go within ten feet or so from the ground. You've done a lot of acrobatics at school. You could climb out the window and down the wheel."

"Now, wait up on that deal, Felicia!" she exclaimed, throwing her hands in the air. "I don't mind doing a lot of things for you, but climbing down a windmill wheel isn't one of them."

"Do you want Nick and his buddies to come back

here and get this map and wire? That's going to happen if we don't get help right away."

Joan sighed deeply.

"I don't know why I have anything to do with you." She sat down and slipped off her shoes. "When we get back to Wellington, you and I have come to a parting of the ways. I don't think I'm even going to speak to you when we meet in the halls."

"Hurry up. Leo's liable to come back any minute and find out you're gone."

She looked up at the window.

"What do I do if I do get down without breaking my neck?" she asked. "How am I going to get help? I don't speak Dutch, and I might not be able to find anyone who speaks English."

"Karlje can write you a note."

"You think of everything, don't you?" Then the smile died in her eyes. "Pray for me," she said seriously.

With that, she climbed up on Felicia's shoulders, reached up, opened the window, and hoisted herself over the sill.

"Here goes nothing," she called down, managing a little laugh.

And then she disappeared from view.

"I didn't know a girl could be so brave!" Steve exclaimed in awe.

"There aren't many like Joan," Felicia said.

She knelt with the two boys in the dust and prayed that God would protect Joan and help her get down safely. They were just getting to their feet when there was a sound at the door.

"It's Leo," Karlje exclaimed fearfully. "Now he'll see that Joan's gone, and we'll all be in a mess!"

They waited breathlessly until the door swung open.

"Uncle Hans!"

"We're so glad to see you," Felicia exclaimed. "How did you get the key?"

"The locks on these doors are old," he explained quickly. "It wasn't anything to open them with a penknife."

"Is that–that Leo still down there?" Karlje asked.

Hans nodded.

"He stopped in and told me not to cause any trouble because he slept light," Hans said. "I kept a watch at the window in the room where they had me, but I did not see him go out. So I know he is still downstairs." There was a short silence. "I saw that girl climb down the wheel."

"Did she make it all right?" Felicia asked breathlessly.

"The last I saw of her she was scooting across the field like a scared rabbit."

"Thank God!" Felicia breathed prayerfully.

"It won't be long until the police are here," Hans said. "You can be sure of that."

* * *

That evening on the Bible Boat, Felicia and Joan were fixing dinner for the two boys and Karlje's Uncle Hans.

"You'll never know how relieved we were when Hans said he saw you drop to the ground and run across the field, Joan," Felicia said.

"You weren't the only one."

Steve snickered.

"I wonder what Leo thought when the police woke him and put the handcuffs on him?"

"Or Nick Sweeney and Jon when they were arrested in Caisse's Artist's Supply Shop?" Karlje added.

"The police said that they found the diamonds right where the map said they would," Hans observed. "So I guess everything worked out after all."

"I don't mind telling you, I'm glad it's over," Joan said.

There was a long, painful silence. Karlje's Uncle Hans squirmed uncomfortably. Two or three times it looked as though he was about to speak, but he did not. At last, he turned to his nephew.

"I've been doing a lot of thinking about what you said to Teunis and Wil in that little meeting you had yesterday, Karlje," he began.

"About Jesus dying to save us from sin?"

He nodded.

"And about Him keeping us from sin." He took a deep breath. "That's my trouble. I don't want to drink and fight and get into trouble. I keep telling myself that I'm not going to do it anymore. But I go right out and do it again."

"That's because Satan rules us and our lives until we confess our sin and let Jesus save us," Karlje explained. "Miss Mabel says that somebody is going to rule us all our lives. If we let Satan do it, our lives are going to be a mess, and we'll wind up going to hell. But if we let Jesus into our hearts and make Him the Master of our lives, we'll serve Him, and we won't be getting into trouble all the time. And–and when we die, we'll go to heaven."

Hans breathed deeply.

"I don't understand what you're talking about," he said finally. "But I'm tired of living the way I have been. Whatever this is you're talking about, I want it."

Karlje stared at him uncertainly. His mouth sagged open in disbelief. His lips trembled as he strove to speak but could not. Then, without saying a word to Hans he turned to Felicia and Joan.

"Come here quick!" he cried. "Uncle Hans wants to be a Christian, and I–I don't know what to do!"

They came in and talked with the distraught Dutch artist, explaining in detail the way of salvation and what the Bible said about sin and the fact that every person needs a Savior. Hans knelt obediently and prayed with them. When he got to his feet, there was a strange look in his eyes.

"You know," he said, "I've been watching Karlje ever since he started coming here to the Bible Boat and became a Christian. There was such a change in him. I've felt for a long time that my life could be different, too, if I'd just do what he did."

* * *

Uncle Hans left the Bible Boat shortly after dinner, proudly carrying the Bible Joan and Felicia gave to him. Steve and Karlje went to bed and were soon fast asleep, and Felicia began to write a letter.

"Who're you writing to?" Joan asked.

"I thought I'd better drop Miss Duncan a line." She handed the paper to her friend.

"Dear Miss Duncan," Joan read aloud.

"I thought I should write and let you know how things are going here. Steve and Karlje haven't been a bit of trouble. In fact, we've found them a big help.

"We planned on doing some sightseeing this week, but all we've done is a little shopping. Joan bought an oil painting for her dad's birthday. . . ."

She stopped reading and looked up, her eyes laughing.

"Written in the true Wellington spirit," she murmured.

THE
FELICIA CARTRIGHT
SERIES

Felicia Cartright, a petite blonde who is one of the most popular students at Wellington School for Girls, has a surprising inclination toward mysteries. If a mysterious situation arises, it either makes its way to Felicia, or Felicia somehow finds it. Though this is a bit trying for her happy-go-lucky roommate, Joan Bailey, it does prevent life from becoming monotonous. It also enables Bernard Palmer, the popular author of the "Danny Orlis" books, to write an entertaining series of stories for girls aged twelve to eighteen.

The mysteries range from a valuable missing antique to an attempt by claim jumpers to steal a deposit of tungsten ore. There's excitement and action galore—but there's also spiritual guidance and blessing because Felicia and her partner-in-adventure love the Lord and take Him into account in all their experiences.